STITCHES & SCARS

poems

Rolland Vasin
(Vachine)

LUMMOX PRESS
SAN PEDRO, CA

Copyright © 2021 Rolland Vasin (Vachine)

All rights reserved. No part of this book may be reproduced without the express written permission of the author, except in the case of written reviews.

ISBN 97809997784-5-6

Library of Congress Control Number: 2019949822

First edition

Lummox Press
3127 E. 6th St.
Long Beach, CA 90814
www.lummoxpress.com

Printed in the United States of America

Cover and Text Design by Dotti Albertine

DEDICATION

For my grandfather, John, the family's founding poet;

for my father, Ray, a newspaper reporter and technical writer during the infancy of aerospace exploration, especially for never missing an opportunity to correct my grammar;

and to my deepest craft critics, Peter J. Harris, Suzanne Lummis, and Ellen Bass, without whose high standards my poetic voice would never be heard or seen.

CONTENTS

Acknowledgments, xiv

Publisher's Note, xv

Part I / WAR
Rancho Mak: Origins of a Naval Officer

City Terrace – 3

1952 – 4

1956 – 5

Confession – 6

Inside Mother's Refrigerator – 7

A Place in the Desert – 8

Leaving Lake Balboa – 10

Conflicted

1960 – 12

1964 Newport – 13

Advanced Calculus – 14

Gangway – 15

Boy – 16

USS Kitty Hawk, South China Sea, 1968 – 18

CV 63 Decomission – 19

Contents

Night Duty Ensign – 20

Seaman Deuce – 22

Cheaper Than Canaries – 23

Portals – 24

PTSD – 25

Invisible Wounds – 26

Bye Bye Mike – 27

Breakfast Song – 28

Unitarian Requiem Denial – 29

Rant – 30

Veteran's Anthem – 31

Vietnam Veteran – 32

Declaration – 33

9/11 – 34

Jumper – 35

Covenant – 36

Urban Sniper Kills 9 – 37

Part II / SOCIAL JUSTICE SUCH AS IT IS

Know Naught – 40

Athens, GA / Summer of Love – 41

Disturbing the Peace – 42

Beat Denizens – 43

God is Blind, Black, and Lesbian – 44

Just Say No – 45

Bear Strange Fruit – 46

Contents

Miles 'n' Trane Blues - 47

MLK, APRIL 4, 1968 - 48

Oh, Shenandoah, After the American Folksong - 49

Next Shoah - 50

Physics of Justice - 51

Prison Colors - 52

Self Defense - 53

Requiem for Mike the Cop - 54

Self-pity - 55

Shadow Players, Refrain - 56

These Walls - 57

Tribute to Motown - 58

What's the Score? - 59

You Amsterdam - 60

Witness - 62

George Carlin—In Memoriam - 63

Last Supper -- 64

Hindrances - 65

Song for V - 66

For Dee - 67

School Massacre - 68

Song for Parkland Children - 69

mother's wallop - 70

Los Angeles Uprising - 71

Life - 72

ICE - 73

Contents

IAMsterdam – 74

How? – 75

Homie – 76

hollywoodland – 77

Family Story– 78

Shall Not Perish – 79

Let Syrians – 80

orlando chorus – 81

Zoo – 82

Trust What is, For Lynn – 83

"Make Fun of People with Handicaps" – 84

A Writing Teacher's Prompt – 85

Lemon Trees – 85

Taps – 86

Christmas Present at Esalen – 87

Christmas Eve, **As Told by the Victim** – 88

Boy Sings in Pawn Shop – 89

Part III / HEARTS BROKEN & OTHERWISE

Beloved – 92

Siciliana – 93

Sex with Anne Sexton – 94

??? Elu – 96

behold shawna – 97

Combustion – 98

Cowboy Jake's Lament – 99

Contents

Dame Noir - 100

All She Wrote, Long and Dry - 101

Draga - 102

Fish Tale - 103

Happy Birthday Daughter - 104

Heavy with Child - 105

How Cat Saved Our World from Germs - 106

How to Write a Confessional - 107

Birmingham Braves - 108

For the Queen of the Pig People - 109

jett plain - 110

Letter to Daughter, Not Mailed - 111

Looks Fade, Intimacy Is Forever - 112

Love Poem #687 - 113

maggie's nipple shadow - 114

Marine Biology 115

Masque - 116

Bad Night for Meat - 117

Pervert - 118

Metrical Feet - 119

My Ex Said - 120

Northern Michigan - 121

Note Found on Marilyn Monroe's Grave - 122

Porch Scene - 123

Recovery - 124

...and Shirley Runs Esalen's Farm - 125

Contents

Garrison Station - 126

Those Things You Don't Do - 127

two cents change - 128

Yama - 130

Polly Vocal's All Girl Band - 131

Pathways - 132

About Times - 133

Skirball Reading Elevator Chat - 134

Bucky & Flo - 135

Prayer - 136

Highland Park Film Festival - 137

Song for Wrinkles - 138

Hurry Up Sailor - 139

Lies - 140

Job Description - 141

Muse - 142

Power Animal - 143

Requiem for a Black Sea Sturgeon - 144

Sabbath Observed - 145

Sacred Space for Flowers - 146

Shadow Players - 147

Stranger - 148

Stuffed Animal - 149

Union Station Ticket Agent - 150

Introvert - 151

Be Right Back - 152

Winter Solstice at Esalen, Big Sur - 153

Samson - 154

Pre - 155

Marriage Sonnet - 156

mama said - 157

Latchkey - 158

"I felt seen for the first time, because I had let myself be seen." - 160

Bleeding Deacon for the Afflicted - 161

"The Smallest Caskets are the Heaviest" - 162

Where Does the Laughter of Children Go? - 164

Denouement - 165

Mercy - 166

Part IV / SELECTED POEMS

Of Places

Lost and Found - 169

Ms. Blizzard - 170

Incomprehensible - 171

Monsoon, Phoenix - 172

Summer Solstice, Indigo - 173

Nature's Game - 174

This Mallorca - 175

cormorant - 176

Oh, Sweet Mother of Christ, - 177

Rountree Lane Workshop - 178

What Our Moon Believes - 178

Inconvenient Truths

Rainy Day - 181

Dark Think - 182

Creed - 183

About Time - 184

Au Bon Pain - 185

Landay for Medusa - 186

Landay for Skater - 187

Tangy Tercets

Marriage - 189

Protect This Child - 190

Window - 191

On the Rocks - 192

1926 - 193

Part V / THANATOS

Poem Appropriated - 196

Last Dream - 197

Mortician - 198

Lance - 199

read some poems at your link - 178 - 200

Contents

PART VI / THE REMAINS

    Route 68 Ballet – 202

    Rountree Lane Sunset – 203

    Industrial Poetry – 204

    How to Write Poetry – 205

    Ambition – 206

    A Child of My Own – 207

    from Zohar – 208

    Buddha Bekins – 209

    Shattered – 210

    High Society – 211

    Gibberish – 212

    Sabbatical – 213

About Vachine

    aka Rolland Vasin – 214

ACKNOWLEDGMENTS

The author is grateful to Lummox Press for publishing *Combustion*, Beyond Baroque Press for publishing *Yama* and Tia Chucha Press for publishing *How and Homie*.

PUBLISHER'S NOTE

First of all, It's an honor to bring the poetry of Vachine to a larger audience. Lummox Press endeavors to publish first timers whose poetry is outstanding, giving them an opportunity for the validation they deserve. In this case, that is an understatement.

The 20th century was fraught with calamity, catastrophe and savagery; all byproducts of technology and discovery mixed with a mad lust for power and greed. It looks like the 21st century is off it's rocker.... or is it the human race that's gone a bit mask crazy? One could think that chaos reigns supreme, at least that's Trump's message. But friends, I don't believe I don't believe it has to be this way. Sure, these scary times yet there is a sliver of hope; there is still a hunger to understand, to eat at a restaurant, to get back to the old ways, to end the monster known as the Corona Virus and get back to our daily lives. I believe that poetry is an essential component to finding that stability.

I'm not a spiritual person in the classical sense but I do believe that we have gotten caught up in a scheme that is hellbent on a simple solution to our troubles. And it is this simplistic longing that creates the demand for a hero. But not the flawless hero of days of old, naw, perfection makes us nervous. What we require is someone like us, who steps up when needed, emerging from the shadows of

Publisher's Note

self-doubt, isolation, depravity, PTSD.... in other words a survivor! We turn to this traveler for the oral history that will help make us whole again. Like the scene in the iconic Samurai movie Yojimbo, where the anti-hero, lone figure, emerges from a cloud of dust to exact justice, in this case it's Vachine who strides purposely towards us; a man who has weathered the best and the worst of the late 20th century and the beginning of the 21st.

He may seem to be broken (and who of his generation can't say the same) but man, can he lay it down!

Ladies and gentlemen, I give you VACHINE.

RD Armstrong
Lummox Press

Part I

WAR

"For as long as Winston can recall, Oceania has been in a constant state of war—with whom it was at war is of neither importance nor consequence."

—George Orwell, 1984

Rancho Mak
Origins of a Naval Officer

City Terrace

My grandparents, Nicodemus and Lucy Makarewich, moved their family from Detroit, Michigan, to Van Nuys, California, because Nick's doctor told him he had three years to live, and perhaps the milder California climate might extend that life expectancy.

Orchard property was purchased in what is now called Lake Balboa, the one-room house was ultimately expanded; then several houses and barns were added, and the compound was named Rancho Mak.

The family was lonely without their Slavic immigrant friends, left behind in Detroit, until a pocket of Ukrainians was discovered in City Terrace, East Los Angeles.

On Sundays Nick and Lucy drove from Van Nuys to City Terrace. The journey was two hours through the verdant San Fernando Valley via Riverside Drive, by a grid of narrow roads—no highways or freeway, just yet.

Graced with the abundant hospitality of folks from the old country, Nick and Lucy's conversation with these new friends proceeded even though dialect separated their full communication. They shared heavy Eastern European meals, galumki, pirozhki, kielbasa, black currant vodka.

Soon, the Ukrainians began driving to Rancho Mak in Van Nuys each Sunday for a feast culled from crops and animals raised on our ranch. Stuffed and sleepy in the living room, I fell asleep on Grandpa's chest, amid the smell of whiskey and sweat, surrounded by the lullaby of Russian-language stories I couldn't understand.

1952

A stand of English walnut trees towered over Grandpa's acreage. Fifty feet straight up we climbed supple boughs. Nine years old, the world to conquer. Spread out below us, an endless canopy, orange, apple, pear, apricot, finger-like branches, deep green leaves bob in the breeze like sign-language cheers for Ike Eisenhower.

1956

The year the street was paved. Before that,
two day's rain and the dirt road was a quagmire.
Cars bondaged into the sucking mud.

Our block was ethnically diverse. We lived
on Grandpa's orchard acreage. Russians,
four wooden houses, lofted barn, chicken pens.

Neighbors were identified by slur, Chinks, Dagos,
Mexicans, but all Anglos called by last name,
The Standards, The Wilsons.

If the mud-anchored cars were abandoned until
soil dried they would be permanently stuck.
Next-door farmer Joe had a small Caterpillar tractor.

Second day of rain, Joe moved the rig onto
the soggy former passageway, pulled mired
autos out and up into their driveways.

Accepted "Thank you" as compensation. Death
in the family? Expect a bucket of fried chicken
and biscuits on the front porch, no questions asked.

Clogged drain, plumber neighbor Howard snaked it out,
wouldn't even take a cold beer—told Dad a few jokes
I didn't get and trudged home in the dark.

Pavement separated this community. Cars sped by,
no more tractor-pulls, no drain clearings, slurs went
underground. Television became the closest neighbor.

Confession

I shot a wren on an apple-tree branch with my BB rifle,
my Christmas gift, the one I scoured the house for until
I saw the gun-box in the broom closet. Santa got my letter.
The wren swung off his perch, into an orchard furrow,

on his back, carcass warm, hazed eyes. I shot another,
then dozens fell on the frosted mantle of Winter. Stray cats
pawed and picked at the tiny bodies. It's always Spring to cats
when death is loose on cultivated fields.

Summer, a sparrow was flopping a loose wing on the lawn.
I wanted to mend it, keep her as a pet. I built a little pen. Held
to my chest, her gyrations amped. My gut clenched at my failure
to mellow her agonal wildness, atone for my Winter serial murders.

I mercied two fingers over the head, flicked my wrist, wrapped
in rags and hid its broken body under other trash in our dumpster.

Inside Mother's Refrigerator

Vessels checked in but didn't check out.
Pickled herring in sour cream with no label
to identify its century of origin,
green cocktail olives from the 1930s, I guessed,
that were no doubt black at some distant past,
milk that soured in one day out of self-protection.

Among, and within, the international choir of half-
or-less-filled containers lived several dozen species
of bacteria, molds, fungi, and as yet unnamed spores,
grown into a rainbow of leafy profusion. No space
available for mayonnaise, Weber's bread, or Strawberry
Crush to tempt the attention of a teenager.

An International Harvester brand freezer-frig-crisper
combination, this particular unit had no knowledge
of the words fresh or crisp.
The fridge's interior could only be considered
nurturing if botulism could be considered nutritional.

As though Depression-era food hoarding remained
in 1963, there being no other apparent explanation
for the gathering storm of bottles, jars, cans, sacks,
Tupperware and Melmac—all partially full
if only with a stain of long-forsaken, formerly edible, objects,
dehydrated and left for whoever was in the greatest need.

A black hole of used food meant to feed the starving,
domestic and foreign, who tramped through
her dining room for their weekly Sunday suppers,
but were never offered the delicacies
from Mother's mausoleum
of deceased sustenance.

Vachine

A Place in the Desert

I

My Grandpa Nick, a Russian-American, built anything.
He held an acre on the flats below Sheephole Mountains
outside Twenty-nine Palms, California. Government-deeded
land, free if a house was built within two years—no strings.
Summers, school holidays, cousins and I inducted into
Gramp's labor camp went, like older guys who got drafted,
to war; we were not given a vote on the pending journey.
Rode in an old green Plymouth, trailer of lumber followed
behind like a faithful dog. A week's sustenance in the cavernous
trunk also took the six-hour night run across Low Desert towns
like Joshua Tree and the Morongo and Lucerne valleys without stopping for
a soda, ice cream, or Cheetos for us convicts.

II

129 degrees on the thermometer, hung in the shade of an outhouse Gramp
built all by himself. Neighbor guy, Ivan, invited us over
in the afternoon highs, had a swamp cooler, big fan evaporation
so only 80 degrees in his one-room warren. Grampa and Ivan spoke
in Russian the rest of an afternoon; we didn't know what they were saying.
I had a hard time staying awake, and shivered too, slipped on a flannel
long-sleeve, dozed until dark, headed back to our home-in-progress.
Coleman-stove-heated kielbasa, beans, sourdough, dipped cookies
into hot Postum. Gramp gave us our next-day plans and after a few
farts we hit the hay. Lay awake in the black, black. We couldn't see our
 hands in front of our face—that kind of dark. Talked about girls, cowboy
heroes, soldier stories our Uncles had told us, but not girl cowboys or girl
soldiers—well, that's another story.

Gramp just listened. We had to stop when his snoring cut in. He didn't snore in Russian so we couldn't just ignore it. In our dreams we prayed for dawn's delay.

III

Well, after a while, us boys all went to that Vietnam War. We came home men of trauma on account of being with corpses that had done nothing to deserve their fates. We don't talk about atrocities with civilians because, if you haven't been there, you've got nothing to say. Grampa had a stroke. In the ICU, in my naval officer uniform, held Gramp's right hand, the one with the half-fingers, stumps that remained after the rest were taken by an uncovered workplace machine. Nurse said he was completely paralyzed. His hand slightly tightened around mine. His steel-blue eyes stared into mine, ever so slight squint of ferocity; tears streaked his white-stubbled cheeks; I knew what he was saying.

Leaving Lake Balboa

Of a Summer eve, walk out onto the back patio, turn west. Orchards are all that's visible, to the horizon. White-barked English walnut, Granny Smith apple, cling peach trees, foliage lush, green in season. Crickets chirp a symphony, percussion by bull frogs at faucets in the irrigation furrows freshly cut by small Cat 'dozer that morning.

My memory of Rancho Mak—acreage, clustered clapboard houses, 1950s San Fernando Valley. The Western boundary was Bull Creek, a dry riverbed, which only bellowed when flash-floods ran the valley floor toward the muddy snake of the Los Angeles River. Over the eons, the little wadi was carved into a deep gorge. Aggregate-gravel palisades, and redolent riverside bushes, fell into Winter's torrent, and the earth's yawn widened.

Even in triple-digit summers, a stream meandered the rocky bottom, provided sipping moments for many furry mammals, attracted predators, hunched on the edges, keen for a fast meal. Velvet darkness and serene dampness from August monsoons sealed a permanent bond between bare feet and sandy loam soil.

In a year during which John Kennedy was President, neighbor boys excavated bones from the river cliff, below Sweny's Ranch. When laid out in an open grazing meadow, the skeleton was of a horse, a disappointment to the boys who rooted for a dinosaur. War in Vietnam soon followed, consumed those boys, through sanctioned murder, or sacrificed limbs, buried and forgotten in random fields like that horse.

Conflicted

1960

We were seventeen in 1960, didn't know Blacks
outside of TV, nor lynch mob, lunch-counter
Jim Crow, had never heard the word rape.
Slid around the gymnasium floor's Sock Hop
with cute White girls, oblivious to Montagnards'
midnight missions from steamy jungle lairs. Knew
hunger only from folk songs; crackers were crushed
into cream of tomato soup; draft—wind under doors.

1964 Newport

Baez and Dylan sing songs of the fight,
mouths thrust forth truth of their might.
Issues were so clear, colors so bright,
before our napalm turned all into night.

Advanced Calculus
November 22, 1963

Cylinder of chalk clacks onto our blackboard,
reverberates off classroom walls. Professor's
brows tighten; he presses a point about his equation,
derived from a matrix of saddle-points, he explains.
Hand flies into space in front of the dusty slate,
index finger like a blunt pink arrow. PA speaker
in UCLA's bell tower crackles. An imperious voice
announces cancellation of this day's classes.
In mid-windup, Prof. grimaces at the loud interruption,
shakes a fist. A student blurts that President Kennedy
was shot dead in Dallas. Professor's shoulders droop,
face slackens, chalk falls from his hand. Mathematics
yields to the shadow of military induction; our careers
drift out the window toward rice paddies and blue oxen.

Gangway

There are so many ways to get hurt on a warship. Constant attention to surroundings, consistent use of safety measures are the only ways to remain whole because flesh and steel are an unforgiving combination and the flesh always loses. I learned to use the safety chains on every ladder in fear of gory traumas which would result from a fall, and given the vast variety of tasks demanded during every moment on board, at sea or not, falls will occur. My fall happened in dry dock, off a gangway onto the pier at the junction where pallets were meant to serve as transit way to the concrete quay but were placed a half inch above the end of the steel plank, invisible and with no railing beyond the end—my instrument of fatherhood, gashed, not gone, still has scars.

Boy

Chiseled names on the Vietnam Wall
holler under my bed for their mothers,
recall me to the South China Sea.

When I left for that war,
Dad, a Navy man,
next to me at the airport,

did not talk, hug, or puddle.
I walked down the jet-way dry,
a member of McNamara's band.

I fought the enemy from a carrier
in the Gulf of Tonkin.
My boy did not want to join this.

He was extracted by forceps
from his mama's uterus,
did not move, did not cry.

The nurse cleared his nostrils
with a tiny basting bulb.
Boy did not want our air.

The doctor yelled
"Breathe."
Boy coughed, then bawled.

Stitches & Scars

Boy made Lego airports, played
Flight Simulator. The Navy didn't call.
His sons free-fell from their mama's womb
in his family room. Boy cried,
his sons cried, wife cried.
They do not hear dead sailors.

Vachine

USS Kitty Hawk, South China Sea, 1968

Supply Boss calls me Commander–Pallets Pacific
'cuz my only combat skill is corralling empty pallets
for cargo transfer from underway provision ships.
Steep decks below, behind crisp Marine guards,
storekeeper counts atomic weapon's spare parts.
But, if a bomb breaks, who is going to fix it?

After dinner, junior-officer buddies gather
on the catwalk to play Find the Sea Snake,
slithering on the slappy surface waves.
Daydreams about the '66 Chevy Convertible
left Stateside, Bob's Big Boy burger 'n fries,
long 10,000 miles to the wife's softer parts.

Cherry incandescence of the jet bomber's
after-burner spreads Christmas cheer,
like a family-room hearth, season's
ornaments of napalm pods hung with care.
Graffitied slogan "Gook" speaks for the mission.
Who speaks for Trang Bang's burning children?

CV 63 Decommission

The ensign is struck,
her engines silenced for now.
Don't Tread On Me, remains.

Night Duty Ensign

Yankee Station, red carrier, 0200 hours.
Four-acre flight deck
of American territory heels to port
into twenty knots of wind.
A fleet oiler inches alongside.

Suction draws the parallel behemoths
toward collision; potential energies
of aviation gasoline and fuel oil
taunt the thermonuclear warheads
in the hold.

Little men in khaki pants and ball caps,
taut faces on the bridges, one hundred feet
off the water, believe they are in control
of 120 tons of floating grey steel.

A twenty-six-year-old ensign known as Commander-
Pallets Pacific arrives on the hangar deck, orders sailors
to manhandle empty wooden platforms,
replace ones borrowed from the alongside ship.

Sea Knight helo-blades chop the humid black
air blanket over Tonkin Gulf. Cargo nets flatten
on the aft elevator, a half-acre of deck drops 50 feet,
flush with the boson's sponson.

Fork lifts do-si-do their loads amidships.
Storekeepers scurry to offload damp cartons,
characters in a six-hour country-bear jamboree
in the lethal Magic Kingdom of the South China Sea.

Forty years later, in a burger joint, Ensign will see a fellow wearing
a ball cap, embroidery, and metal insignia, a Vietnam Veteran.
Ensign's tears will salt his burger.
He will stare out the window so no one can see him cry—
never told anyone he is afraid the ships will collide, bombs
will explode, he will be in the water being burned alive
by gasoline and fuel oil.

Alone to his fate, he will feel shame
for his weakness. Will have no right
to burden others with these flashbacks,
because he thinks other vets suffer pain
every day but they know how to keep
it to themselves.

Ensign will be powerless over outbursts.
He will write a poem to share the terror,
to keep the .45 out of his mouth just
one more sunshine day.

Seaman Deuce

When a sailor dies fighting his warship,
his mother will never hold him again.
Whether purging vapor in avgas voids,
or fire suppression, a gun is not necessary
for removal of his life; it's still combat—
he has a mission, that duty killed him,
his mother will never hold him again
father will never shake his hand again,
sister will never set him up as icon again,
brother will never brag on him to buddies again...

Cheaper Than Canaries

Sailors inspect vapor-purged voids
used for aviation gasoline.
Asphyxiated, they cry for mama.
She does not save her young men.
Their corpses demand answers.

A thousand gallons of whiskey,
the Twelve Steps,
love of a good woman,
a pistol for breakfast,
do not stop their questions.

Trust God, clean house, help others.
These answers weigh anchor on oblivion.
Desire to punish abandoned,
forgiveness follows.
This ship is not built for harbors.

Vachine

Portals

Knuckles rap on the front door, Naval Officer on the porch,
sharp-creased blues, folded flag under gold-striped sleeve.
Ushered to the front parlor, seated on the worn divan with small
chocolate stains on the taupe cushion, Lieutenant clears his throat,
says Seaman Malone was killed in a riverine-force firefight.
Offers his sorrow for the loss of the family's elder son.
Hands an unopened letter to the sailor's mother.

Mother is left with a flag and a faux-parchment scroll, the spawn
of colicky nights, first steps, pre-school counselors, high school prom,
body-shop repair bills, and all those silent moments when their eyes
locked gaze.

Dear Mom

If you are reading this letter it means
I didn't make it home from 'Nam.

If God took me before you woke I
pray your tears the Lord to take.

Give little Jimmy a hug from me.
Hold him like I was there.

You tell Dad I love him.
I wasn't able to say that myself.

Sell my Corvette to the lowest bidder
so he can run wild with the horses.

PTSD

Corpses pile inside me,
beneath cold decks,
between napalm canisters
and nuclear weapons spare parts.

Red Shirt blown off the flight deck,
ejected pilot's broken neck
asphyxiated Avgas sailor,
held drum-tight by gallons of Scotch.

Deep in the shadows, the Wall's
chiseled warriors cry evil-eye drops.
I hurry up the trail, into sunlight,
until names are only ankle-high.

Humid afternoon, Psych Rehab lobby,
Medevac helicopter chops my sobs.
Jack-knifed on my knees,
I pray to stop hearing blades.

Invisible Wounds

After the wards, some of us vets break into poetry,
in the dim hours when our sobs return for what was lost.

Next week I'll turn seventy-one if I make it until Thursday
On a disability pension from the VA for war-related causes,

last year you could hear me declaring I would never
be caught writing a love poem, or one about daffodils.

This year I've written one of each without a lightning strike.
Another first, I spread bird seed on the lawn around my trees.

Lucky I no longer hear dead sailors cry for mama under
my bed at night, but I spend most of Memorial Day weeping.

A few of my ill brothers rampage, shoot people they don't know
like those they dusted in combat when they were taught no other choice.

Other tortured souls may suicide after flashbacks of past killing deeds
if they remain untreated for replays as sole actor in a Wes Craven film.

Whenever anyone reaches out for help at the last house on the block
I want the hand of recovery always there, and for that I am responsible.

Bye Bye Mike

Mike, the Cop, died today at the VA.
In final days we sat opposite his wheel
chair, retold our Vietnam stories, again.
Swords held high, defenders of freedom
that no longer exists, no one cared about
sacrifices for our country, our mother's.
I'm next off this coil, a trip to my knees
for relief, a Jew who never kneels to pray.

Breakfast Song

In the old days I slept
with a loaded .45.

Meditation made leeway
past trigger.

Haven't slept as well
since disarming.

Unitarian Requiem Denial

Uncle passed a couple years back,
he was a Corpsman in two wars,
saw things no one need ever see.

VA terminated his pension in error.
Took years to get it back.

Add PTSD, another service-related ill.
I took Uncle to Psych
Eval. He described birthing babies
for starving mothers in Korea. Watched
them toss the newborns under trains.

Uncle sobbed without shame,
became a nice guy after his confession, kindly,
of service to residents of his assisted
living home. His parents' church refused
him a memorial plaque—for avowed atheism.

Rant

I left our Vietnam War in '71,
mourned at The Wall in '86.
In between, swam whiskey seas.
Today I grieve each day's dead.
Seaman, corporal, captains, all.
Soldiers, sailors don't kill people.
Governments kill people.

Veteran's Anthem

My song has teeth,
hoarse dawn chant.

Breakfast of enmity,
cold toast, and mouthed barrel.

Knee-view and clasped hands
offered for the collection basket.

Any day above ground
is a good one. No promises
for tomorrow.

These lyrics rub their backs
on my scars like a bear
against a tree.

Live bark embeds
in the fur of conscience.
My song has teeth.

Vietnam Veteran

Discharged, homeless. Nobody
looks through my weathered crow's feet.
They spit on my shadow, from behind.

None uses my name, or touches me
in my cardboard box.
Even your police wear rubber gloves.

I was not resisting arrest.
I just did not comprehend.
You beat me until dead.

Declaration

With PTSD you learn to get ready for impact
at any turn: the backfiring of a car, the popping
of a balloon, or fireworks for a graduation party.
Thanks to the man who I consider the world's
greatest therapist I have become stronger.
Not better, but stronger.
—Adrianne Haslet-Davis, Boston Marathon Bombing Victim

Not better, but stronger. Come around a corner too fast
on me and you can experience the troll who still lives
in a dim corner of my self, the legacy of my war.
Some ask if I've changed meds when my emotions take
full control. I don't use meds. My salvation comes from
my faith, community, service, and the knowledge
of paragraph 15b of my Job Description as Human Being,
which includes a Declaration of Imperfection.

9/11

Seems like a cornball stunt
when a blonde boy at Ground Zero

releases the eleven white doves
that signal our loss of liberty's essence.

The birds' wing beats, an affront to
the tent-auction of grief-swings.

A wrinkled woman's nose honks
like a klaxon call to battle stations.

Our mood elevates as the flock rises;
their flutters muffle the audience's sobs.

Open hands ease into others,
puzzled pieces, a seamless fit.

Jumper

When death is breathing in your face,
like a drunken uncle, when the sweep
of doom is so present it leaves brush
marks on your cheeks, when you are
on the 107th floor, flames and smoke
claiming the space, then you will know
what it is to be a jumper. The leap is
messy, a teenager's room strewn, like
a tour bus wreckage on an icey highway.
Freeze-frame photo: a shirtsleeve man
plummets, head first, from the North
Tower; another man and woman pitch
through fire-blown-out window panels,
somersault together in resonant loving
harmony, a hazy cloud when they hit
the pavement so hard there is only pink
mist above where their bodies should be,
all there is left for the family to take home,
one shoe. A minister said his son who
chose the window was burning in Hell;
his sister said God doesn't love him less.

Covenant

American blood flows from Gettysburg to Shanksville
mixed in raucous union. From Plymouth's Mayflower
to the Golden Door, we never sink, never cower.

Black-White-Gay-Jew-Jap-Yorican Sisters and Brothers
did not go down easy in these killing fields. Their death
by fragmentation cannot hallow this ground.

Nation's destiny manifests sunny on each grassy hill,
not divided against itself, a crucible without a spill.
American blood flows from Gettysburg to Shanksville.

Urban Sniper Kills 9

Since discharged from the War
the soldier only played video games
at his folks' home, in the old room.

His Dad said, "I'm not worried.
He'll snap out of it."
Father was not in the line of fire.

Part II
SOCIAL JUSTICE SUCH AS IT IS

"Artists are here to disturb the peace."

—James Baldwin

Know Naught

Seventeen in '60, didn't know Jim Crow,
never heard the word rape, or of Sather Gate.
Slid around the school's gym floor, Sock Hop
girls slim and fair, oblivious to Montagnard's
midnight missions from steamy jungle lairs.

Athens, GA
Summer of Love

White rhythm and blues obscure parades
of Ivory Coast currency herded up gang
planks, shackled Brothers, Sisters walked

bone-whipped Middle Passage, blood pools.
Bound with barbed wire, jumper cables.
Balls burnt black, Brothers walked.

Forearm across Sister's throat, gingham skirt.
Shins against thighs, penetration against will.
Another mouth to feed crow. Sisters walked.

1968 Peachtree Street, sidewalk rain-walkers,
no shucking, no jiving, no yas'ms, equal
opportunity foreclosures. Color-blind evictions.

Storm moves on through; dewy torch singer
solos her bottomless Blues, like a held elevator,
waiting for the Reverend King's call.

Disturbing the Peace

What a great name for a band:
musicians,
poets,
protesters,
If it ain't broke, break it!

Beat Denizens

Like Bishop petroglyphs,
down dogs smoke ice
creams, chant Howl on
North Beach sidewalks.
Beat, cool, low beret
bearers, zigzag eaters,
finger snappers, synced
for coil-shuffle morals,
fall by hungry i buffet.
Fellow-traveler Trotskyites
under blacklist t-shirts
march backward in their wait
for jazz riffs' return home.

God is Blind, Black, and Lesbian

Blind, so that you'll say "Thank you"
when you see Creation. The mulberry,
citron, pine forest, light from sunshine,
thank you. Black, since only adversity
knows community. A Sappho God, alone
knows what each woman wants. Her vagina
is no less magnificent because she prefers
another woman to eat it, never thinks
any ass is too big. I want her grasp on
my elbow, say just to me,
"There, there, it gonna be all good soon, chil'.
You jus' tell me what's a pesterin'."

Just Say No

A single mother
raising children
would, when confronted
with the prospect
of a new man in her life,
do well to ask herself
if she is committed
to raising yet another child.
Not bearing a child again, but
doing all that's necessary
to launder his skidmarks.

Bear Strange Fruit

The right kind of tree must be chosen.
Strong limbs, of course, must stand separate
from other trees, with enough space for
spectators to gather, shoulder to shoulder,
tall enough so the watchers look up
as though to Calvary, see the dark shape
sway, command attention to the dangler's
misdeed. A tree whose bones are not brittle,
which bear weight of newly blossomed fruit, supple
to withstand forked flicks of vigilante tongues,
fanned like prairie flames to lick at Satan's soles.

Miles 'n' Trane Blues

Trumpet bends the wind,
sax honks in on the downbeat.

Bass duck walks, dah-boom, bah-doom.
Rim shots chop-chop, chop-chop.

Keyboard chords off the refrain
like yellow crime scene tape.

Slinky sister croons a loner's tune
behind her powdered shiner.

Cymbals shimmy her sequined gown.
Strange fruit falls past her golden tooth,

Miles wigs to Tunisia shore.
'Trane pig farms another impro

Says he can't stop the show.
Trumpet Man lays it on the Cat

"Take the horn outta your mouth, Bro."
'Trane trips out to the soiled lands.

Cuts them down from willow boughs.
Miles tunes in to the witness stand.

"If I only had thirty minutes to live
I'd spend it strangling a White Man."

MLK, April 4, 1968

Hold my hand up to the mountain-top.
What did we negotiate? We saw
two inches nearer the Promised Land.
Preach with me the dark of our beasts.

Then you will fear none, tho I'll not
be with you. Sing, that a right is not
a right if a man can take it away. Know
that peaceful means to seek redress
can only end in violence.

The swift bullet of hate silences my jaw,
pierces my spine, when His chariot swings
low over Memphis's balcony of Lorraine.

Oh, Shenandoah
After the American folksong

Oh, rolling river how much blood is on Millwood Plantation?
To which tree was Powhatan tied and bayoneted?
Which poplar was hung with strange fruit?
You know all this, and bear it silently along to the sea.

The gray-ghost patriots at McDonald's know this too,
held under their ball caps, warm, close to the knowledge
of who burned John Mosby's horse.
Can you hear the mamas bawlin'? Can you hear the daddies moan?

Oh, take uncle's ashes, add his tears to theirs.
Release his memories of starved newborns,
tossed 'neath coal trains' wail,
bound away, 'cross the wide Missouri

Vachine

Next Shoah

Shoah's shadow falls on me every day.
After my son's Bar Mitzvah I trained him
in the use of large-caliber firearms.
There will be no next Shoah for him.

After my daughter's Bat Mitzvah I took her
to the Windstar Conference where we learned
the practice of think globally, act locally.
There will be no next Shoah for her.

Physics of Justice

A bully always gets his ass kicked.
It's a cosmic principle, like gravity.
Someone or something bigger shows
up and hurts the bully back, or a big
machine crushes the oppressor flat.
Or, he dies a horribly painful death.
Those kinds of things always happen
'cuz what goes around, comes around,
and it picks up speed on the way back.

Prison Colors

Inmates in uniforms the color of sky they can't see.
First names only, my first poetry lesson for them
begins with Bukowski, syntax of the brutal closer
to their own. Distrust on each face sourced in
ancient trauma, belt buckled, drunken punches.
No matter, I tell them all will be published poets
at workshop's end. They look at me; frozen chops
mask oceans of disappointment told in rapsheets.
Poet calling self Young Pak cops to his sheet, calls life
outside interrupted his own fault, unlike others'
arguments on technicalities. All poems in Hallmark
rhyme chapbook-bound distributed to their families.
Go home triple doors released horizon to horizon
puffers only for the free to roam.

Self Defense

"...killed by racism and gun laws"

When a person is a concealed-carry, the ground
they are standing is measured by muzzle velocity,

boundary of the court of public opinion,
until that scene crosses the victim's threshold.

The issue is not that killers are armed,
but that their victims are not armed.

Requiem for Mike the Cop

Tick tock says the clock,
Mike is dead it knocks.
Reaper pulls the chocks
under the Cop's dock.

Tick tock before the chime
sounds for me, it's time.
Pull my covers,
drop that dime.
Hands walk the Vietnam wall
like a mime.

Mike the Cop bit the dust
his memory begins to rust.
My pit's below the thrust
of death's soiled crust.

Self-pity

When I tie my fortunes
to your falling star,
I land in Alabama,
a feathered Jew,
covered in tar.

Shadow Players, Refrain

Roses are bled
Violence, code blue.
Da Judge done laid down a TRO
directed especially at you, Yo.

These Walls

These walls hold hunger and hurt, fall off your chair
laughter, crossing Jordan heartache from loss
of our baby, sorrow from smack, this world stage
of the dark soul, repossession of stuff and dignity;
these have tears of cry that won't stop.

Down on my knees, part of me dies,
even my breath don't come to the funeral.
These walls are painted in shades of crow.
Some folks just don't have care like they should,
and that shows up on these walls, a stain
in the shape of a parish people want to leave.

No self-help in these walls, the only help hereabouts
is We Help. With the Lord's help, however you hold
a Power Greater Than Yourself in your heart, or not—
maybe it's only confidence that together we're gonna
be OK, because it happened before, or not.
We don't know but we believe these walls.

Tribute to Motown

No Brothers or Sisters in the cruise ship's
Show Lounge production. I walk out
after three numbers. There's a formula
for Motown. First you kidnap Africans
from their villages and sell them as slaves
to Americans who beat, rape, murder,
exploit, maim, demean, and torture them
for about, oh say, four hundred years.
Then you turn them loose on their own
for about another hundred years, still
continuing the abuse.

Then you systematically deny them
citizenship rights, and kill some more
when they assert those rights. You deny
them their native culture, their music, their
dance, their self-expression. But God don't
let only that happen.

He leads Brothers and Sisters be percussion, be
jazz, be soul, be flyy. And,
when those souls swing, and sway, and tap,
and writhe, something comes out their mouths
in melodious blood, and that be Motown.

What's the Score?

October Sunday shadows roll
like velvet into night over LA
hillside family room parquet.

Big TV banners every game final,
every missed shot, each bad call.
Sports page by-liners peacock replays.

Discarded newspaper
cold on hearth bricks.
Old news, in dead ink.

Chips and salsa bowls drained to scraps.
Every score that was going to count
has already marched,
sacrificed to heartburn.

Empty bellies in downhill 'hoods
growl from a daily diet
of 9mm grain boiled in mama's tears.

Their box score's counted in toe-tags,
filtered through crack pipes,
behind iron gates rusted from piss, blood,
and spilled milk.

The radio choir wails in metallic tones
"a motherless child… a long ways from home"
as sharp to the tongue as bitter to the grave.

"No one's gonna save you 'cept yo faith,
'cept yo faith" the chant sways
through the torn screen door.

You Amsterdam

Children in those cobbled streets jeered, "Jew-killer!"
German parents held your girly nine-year-old hand,
pretended the pall of Shoah's shadows did not fall.

You told that fifty-years-ago story
at our Tuesday Witness meeting. I felt
your shame through your hand in mine
during the closing prayer written
by an unknown prisoner in
concentration camp, left on the body
of a dead child:

Let all the fruits which we have bought,
thanks to our suffering from those of ill will,
be their forgiveness.

I abandoned the desire to punish.
You harvested my rain, filled your cistern,
when I cried at the Yom Hashoah memorial.

Our tears nurtured new vines, curled 'round
our legs, heads upward, stretched for sunlight,
lips open, our tongues danced an afternoon waltz.
We slept like nested dolls under silk sheets,
bathed in Hillman, Nietzsche, Carlin and Wilbur.

I cuddled your laughter on my chest,
stroked flaxen hair. We braided
songs from fibers of child-hurt,
I chanted your praise from Proverbs.

Stitches & Scars

My night visits from minion's ashes released
into the custody of your downy-soft ear. Dropped
all inquiries into motive and widened my dawn gaze.
Our entwined selves, like a matted tango
of river reeds, dammed Holland's tidal flows,
held up against another Shoah.

Witness

The Russian cabbie in Sydney taxis
into his rearview that I'm a friendly person,
says every American he knows is pleasant.

Blue eyes ask why my government
is so murderous? I mirror back: Good people
do evil when they cross paths with patriotism.

He squints then why don't Americans speak out?
What I don't tell him is how blue jazz
and yellow dogs, in Leimert Park,
pinned balls on this honky,
how the Anansi Brothers,
with a smile and a Jesus-wrench,

forged 'round kitchen ovens, baking
peach cobbler sweeter from rotten fruit,
eased back the bolts of my armor,
let light slip through
a tiny crack. I say, "I'm a poet,
I speak out, not many listen."

George Carlin
In Memoriam

His sadness for the down and
out, asleep on city sidewalks,
pours, not from a bleeding heart,
but from points of a moral compass.

Last Supper

Witnesseth
foot wash
bread bless
wine drink
G-d thank
psalm sing
hand wring
served upon
Judas's silver

Hindrances

Slaves-in-training herded to harbors,
bone-shackled to wooden ships.

Cat-o-nine tails swung low
rowing over Jordan.

Split backs' bright blood milestones
of bondage's warrant.
Buddha ate meat after the Middle Passage.

Song for V

Created by God in the old way. Rutted face of Olduvai,
braided dreads coiled on the back of her coconut noggin,
flashy olive eyes behind flickered black lashes. Chock full
of loving-kindness, her lips are thick 'cuz she can't kiss fast
enough to pass mama-joy.

A voice that melts like butter on mother's soda biscuits,
chants the Blues so bad I don't know whether to shit or go blind.
Blues from the Serengeti, Middle Passage, Detroit, Blues,
like a torch from bottled gas under chicken in the breadpan, blue.
Mistress of Funk for the darkness, where not even a night light
chases away wreckage of the future.

Funk that interrupts slumber to flirt with us, so we hang,
wait for her choice. She picks none, leaves the room full
of hearts sunken so low we hobble like our pants dropped,
tap the amphetamine-Watusi, scorch sorrow's dance floor.
Philosophers call this existential loneliness, but to brothers
and sisters just a frozen hole in the middle-gut, thawed only
when wet eyes meet, and our choir push-horns Gospel.

For Dee

Only two men ever said they loved me.
Ernie from AA, Dee Black from here.

Not my Dad, or uncles, that's another story
When I lost Ernie to a self-inflicted pistol
shot to his head my faith was tested, didn't
want recovery. When Dee crossed over,
my faith was dented again. Lord, why do
you take the righteous, I asked on my knees?

Michael D, Juwanza, Connie, Dee
in the back, Peter J, A. K., V Kali
over there, Degnan Brothers, a Sister—
not a bitter lot, not swayed by winds
of revenge—they give it up for us
in verse, poem is their hymn. Their
mighty swift sword parses mumbles'
pocket. Gospel according to film at 11.

Dee eased back the bolts of my armor
with a smile and a Jesus-wrench, forged
in family kitchens, baking sweet peach
cobbler from rotten fruit. The least I can do
is chant these words where they will be heard,
strain them through my tears for the dead asleep.
All eyes, shiny like red marbles, glow as we weep.
On the World Stage wall Miles blows taps.

School Massacre

Small coffin lowered into each grave.
List of names the only remains, dust
trails off a Summer-baked road,
hollowed-out sugar-plum fairies,
Oreo crumbs on silken pillows blown
off course, raspberry-skinned knees,
tassels on college mortarboards, stilled.
Who will unwrap bright holiday gifts?
What mirth will turn off vacancy signs?

Song for Parkland Children

Folks drove kids to school today
they came home dead, on NBC.
Two bullets ripped the hearts;
a third, the heads; shot from
the neighbor's guns.

CNN
On the screen,
car pools to blood pools,
slick sound-bites at eleven,
babies on gurney-bridges to heaven.

ABC
Over tented shrouds soiled, caked and stiff,
mamas' wails lift, but make no sense,
drowned by ambulances'
careening indifference.

CSPAN
Gun activists like kneeled nuns' necks
stiffened to God, chant the right to bear
arms shall not be abridged, but mean
the right to raise kids shall.

mother's wallop

upside the head was all she could do to save sonny's life
her great black hope for life after the teen years when most
in the neighborhood gang pass before thirty of a prison
knife fight or some such fate in baltimore. hardwired
for nurturing the issues of her bounty mama is powerless
over the ghetto's vortex to oblivion no way out but school

Los Angeles Uprising

I bought guns,
felt like a boy who lost his mother
in the supermarket. Aisles on fire,
no ollie-oxen-free zone.

At the gun store,
the holstered clerk warned me
that a pistol-grip shotgun
could break my wrist.

She sold me a hunting rifle
with telescopic sight used to kill
grizzly bears.
Santa Monica has no bears.

Only thing breaking
in my town was the TV news,
didn't need the gun. No call
for shooting a cross-haired Angeleno.

My wife didn't get two-fisted armed.
Women with brooms joined
a post-riot brigade, swept ashes
from burn-zone streets.

Life

Pro-choice wants to kill before birth,
pro-life wants the births so babies can die
in foreign wars—the debate is about timing.

ICE

I don't know if Grandma was Documented.
Her Sunday fried chicken was not a rapist,
biscuits had no priors, gravy no rapsheet.
Her home town, in Romania, wanted her
gone, her mother said "Run, never say you're
a Jew;" even the electro-shocks didn't loosen
her nugget of cruel roots, but did kill her.
Her son, aka Dad, was fearful; wouldn't
you be too if you knew you were marked?
It's like Chosen, but fatal in the end—kinda
like involuntary deportation beneath six
feet of Mother Earth so he wore leather
gloves in the get-away car, a 42-horsepower
Hillman Minx, couldn't do mountain passes,
vapor-lock they called it, high in those piney
woods of Flagstaff. He commenced to rolling,
didn't stop 'til we tossed his ashes, kept in a
Crown Royal sack, out the Cessna's rear window,
into Santa Catalina's channel, he never liked fish
on account of his dentures, but that's another story.

Vachine

IAMsterdam

I saw the Dam, heavy stones and mortar,
set between tidal floods and canal-side houses.
For one home's tour, I stood behind
two New Jersey Jewesses,
big dyed hair and diamonds.

Projected on the wall, an old newsreel,
a wave of Blackshirts marching in a stadium.
The Fuehrer's thin arms flail above his podium.
On the opposite wall, the film's flicker animates
Anne Frank's portrait.

At my elbow, a toothy, blond,
blue-eyed son, cherub-white face,
Ranonkel on his nametag,
snaps a sieg-heil salute.

His teacher hurls a finger of scorn in his face.
Loose diamonds fall through the oven grate.
I can't breathe for the odor of burnt hair.

Hard rain falls on me all day.
Copper gutters overflow.
Pallid gulls in Dam Square are soaked
and will not fly.

I cannot love Ranonkel, nor herd his city's waters.
No choice but to pray for willingness
to hold bricks in the dike against the next Shoah.

How?

If a boy of Japanese ancestry from Gardena was sent with his parents to a concentration camp in Wyoming for the duration of World War II, and, upon arrival, his baseball bat was confiscated, so he never played baseball again,

if a brother and sister from Boyle Heights were jeered as Mexicans, and told to go back to where they came from, but they and all their Indigenous ancestors, far back as anyone could count, came from Boyle Heights,

if a black girl from Mississippi watched her father dragged from his house in the middle of the night, by men in bed sheets, hanged on a poplar tree and his mutilated body set on fire with gasoline, so every time she fills the tank of her car in South-Central, and smells gas, she sees her Dad on the tree,

how do these citizens abandon the desire to punish their tormentors long enough to earn a Nobel Peace Prize, be confirmed as a Justice of the Supreme Court, or just finish school?

How do we move from them to we? How do we embrace as family? How do we all say "God Bless America"?

Homie

Smokes a Camel and spits on the asphalt. Wife-beater
under hoodie, gordo brother's pants, legs cut to fit.
Holy Mother of universal exultation holds the cathedral's
door, but there's no road in the shadow of her wings.
Mama's cancer, relief from Dad's Spirited belt buckle,
unanswered prayers. Must blaze his own trail across
Zanja Madre. Sun roasts the air above LA River bridges.
Smog hangs with charcoal smoke from San Gabriel's wildfires;
acrylic sunset paints the Heights in oranges and lemons,
like crime scene tape. Thirst quenched by Colt 45, moist
night grasses of Plaza De La Raza, he curls down on damp sod.
Dream song lyrics are punctuated by chingada between syllables.
Hollenbeck Division putos in rubber gloves sweep the park,
Waistband 9 the only peace he's ever known.

hollywoodland

bastard child of greasy spoons rubbed in a rusted chevy
umbilical back to east jesus michigan neon pink hair
bird legs scissor south on cherokee skin tight sheath
no underpants caboose so skinny theres scant room
for boulevard johns rear alley door ticket man cash box
peep show beverly hills eyelashes beckon above van nuys
hook mouth hungry for childhood lost to dynamite fishing
baseball bats belly up dead on arrival manners fell off
on highway 40 barstow question is why pimps suck wings
at popeye's on cahuenga sneers baited for next mamas girl
when they all end up jane-doe-tagged at county general

Family Story

"The phrase 'dysfunctional family' is redundant." —Anon

He beat up his sister, but
didn't hit her in the face,
just in case she wanted to
get married, someday. He,
right afterwards, was taken
straight to LA County Jail.
And, she hasn't talked to him,
ever, in several decades,
nor has he been drunk, even once.

Shall Not Perish

Southbound on U.S. 101, news radio reports
another school massacre. An odd-looking airplane
climbs and banks, lumbers out of the Van Nuys airport.

I almost hit the center divider staring at its configuration,
straight wing span, pods in the front of the wings—
weird place for jets. Wait, those are propellers glinting
in the sunlight—a vintage DC-3 drones over my car.

Like the plane, I'm the sole survivor of my ancestors
We are ancient structures, still sleek and functional,
claiming our place in the afternoon, yet outward bound 'cross
that celestial sphere of time like the victims of the Holocaust.

We Jews are fortunate not to have the clutter of heaven or hell
added in our worries. All that forever remains are memories
of loved ones' deeds, celebrated annually, on their date of passing.

Let Syrians

settle in Detroit.
Rusty mufflers torn around
the block too many times.
Headlights brighter for escape.
Bombed-out houses left for dead
reoccupied. Mothers nurse
babes between shifts.
American Labor yearns to breathe free against
all odd bigots, storms, bandits.

Why not them? Have we
forgotten our grandfathers'
blood?

orlando chorus

occurs when birds sing at the start
of a new day, to attract a mate
or to call in the whole flock.
there is no good sense singing at night,
because it's hard to see through the dark.
after the killing stopped, and before
coroners arrived, there was a profound
absence of sound, except for the chirp
of cell phones of the dead, the tangle
of limbs as sensual as live dances
before rifle and pistol assault; ring-tones
announce departures at the gates of soul.

Zoo

The gorilla throws his shit
at the crowd. Popcorn flies
in all directions.

My stomach is tight with laughter,
on the level above the throng,
my hands on the railing,

beside an ice cream cart, with its umbrella
selling America, underneath eucalyptus
branches, enslaved from Australia.

My heart beats in slow motion,
light-headed in the Bay's humid air,
far from serenity.

Threw his shit like a husband's rage
at a cheating wife.
I interview Mr. Gorilla.

Says he feels Black, tainted, moody,
misses the matted dampness of fallen
leaves, vines moldy on the forest floor,

tangled to trip up pursuers as they clamber
the slopes of Kilimanjaro,
seekers of fortunes in new slaves.

Pounds his chest; the sound of thunder
makes my knees knock.
He needs a hug, his mate in Africa.

Trust What Is
For Lynn

Well I'll tell you, my pain belly is still full up
from our last encounter, so any more will spill
over to anguished bellows from intestinal sources,
like those heard in a supermarket when small
children are separated from their mothers,
and all they know is existential loneliness,
on steroids, shared with the entire population
of eager shoppers playing Big-box bumper carts.
Tykes abandon trust, unable to bear their truth
felt in the deepest chakras, their only in-the-now
awareness the weighted blanket of the drowned.

"Make Fun of People With Handicaps"
A Writing Teacher's Prompt

I laughed when I saw a disfigured person.
Mother knuckled my face. Told me not to
make fun of them—"They can't help it."
That cheek still stings.

I wore a Happy Face until dead sailors swam
across the Whiskey Sea, jumped me
in psychiatric wards, took away
my normal looks.

My tribe, afflicted since the apple,
welcomes the handicapped.
All the more hands for harvest.
No hands? Use your feet.

Lemon Trees

Can't go out for a burger, drop
a few fruits on the way home and hope the seeds produce
a tree, maybe a grandchild.
Is that asking too much?
God knows there are enough
seeds in the orb to get things
started, but it's a stationary tree,
has to rely on birthing conditions
in its immediate vicinity, fret
that mobile animals don't spirit
away the ova. The four-leggers
aren't so bad 'cuz their poop
returns seeds to the soil. But
the two-legged buggers are a worry.
They do weird things. No telling fates
of the tiny future trees embedded
in the tart pulp beneath bitter skin,
plucked out like offending face hair,
tossed into landfills under toxic
debris, plastic, iron, methane gas.
Even a socialist president can't help.

Taps

Death penalty sentences for warriors and their fathers'
God and country rushes by ears deaf to danger
of passage to unnamed graves.
The bugle sounds.

Admirals depend on strict compliance for retention
of shoulder stars and white toilet seats.
The bugle sounds.

Sailors expire in voids hollering for mamas who
support boys fallen to fires from faulty ordnance.
The bugle sounds.

The pilot's neck crushes upon ejection through a canopy
not blown but missions must go on.
The bugle sounds.

58912 chiseled names on a black granite wall
the shade of darkness in each family's memory.
The bugle sounds.

A mass-murderer's death sentence yields decades
of solitary daily meals, books, TV, and letters from
admirers.
No bugle sounds.

Christmas Present at Esalen

I am a Jew.
Christmas scares me.
I did not kill the Prince of Peace.
I don't feel guilty yet fear for my life
on all His annual remembrance days.
I put my leather shoes out on the deck of Big Yurt
for when I needed the detached toilet room. I placed
the shoes near the railing onto which I held while slipping
on my loafers when nature called. During our yurting
rain had fallen. When I let myself out of the room
headed to the loo my shoes had been moved
under the eaves keeping them dry, away
from the water pouring off the roof
onto the railing. That's the best
Christmas present
I ever got.

Vachine

Christmas Eve
As Told by the Victim

Still, still snow drifts up. Roses hunker
against stone walls. City streets are on fire.
Shadow people flicker behind flames.

Barrel pressed below my jaw. Muzzle
rigid on my artery. My face pressed
to cement for rear entry. Organ tissue
tears. The gentleman asks my age.
I give a younger number so I'll be
more worthy of raping. Quickly
as takedown blossoms, his storm
surge subsides to faint odors.
Weapon withdrawn without prejudice,
he shares it's not personal. I thank him.
Cops ask me what I was wearing. A sister
visits to cleanse wounds. She asks
how I am feeling. I make sounds like
nails in the grammar of Jesus.

Boy Sings in Pawn Shop

His blues reach down down
beyond the howdys
fake smiles and civil tongue
down below parental duty
god and country vehicle code
down below where she hurt me
that will never heal even lower
to the chaos of hurt that has no
name won't ever be spoken no
light filters to that trench down
below bottom where salvation
has too many syllables yanks
that tear oyster core up
out onto the counter top
of my transactions all
it can do is quiver

PART III
HEARTS BROKEN & OTHERWISE

"Deep inside the misery of daily life,
love lies bleeding."

—Tony Hoagland

Beloved

Lakes chuckle when she walks
their shores.
Homeless feel fed even before
she wheels them chow.
Crowds suckled by her smile
long before she presses flesh.
Accelerant of well-being.
No one owns her sustenance.
Harp or sword draws her near.
Stake a claim, she disappears.

Siciliana

Cuddle me, sing your ass off only with me.
Aim melody hard into my curls.

Strum my trigger, peel me from our ceiling.
Show me around town, my ass tight in basic-black.

Sin pillows on my chest jiggle, points arc
in the Square of Our Saints, ignore their stone boners.

Pluck my spot with tight lips. Clamp my nipples
to the bed-post. Don't worry about your space in heaven.

All the electric guitars are in the other place.
Slide me four fingers while I evil-eye your mother's picture.

When I come loudly, village lights will dim,
and she'll call you home, for supper.

What's age anyway? My creases are underrated,
that's where eros has set up residence.

Sex with Anne Sexton
(Inspired by Billy Collins' "Taking Off Emily Dickinson's Clothes")

I earn each splinter of tenderness you surrender
from your trauma-veined heart. I strike flinty
shards of sentiment with my tiny pimp-hammer
forged in Mama's kitchen.

It's like trying to chisel a wafer of nurture
from a concrete post with a dull screwdriver
and a banana for a hammer. I nibble on
the crumbs of your narcissism, while you
buff your crimson nails.

I drive pitons into the monolith of your neglect,
pray for a stranglehold on your gaze, a trickle
of affection from your dry gulch.

Efforts to sluice out your love stiffens
my resolver but your wry smile wafts
away my ardor, like a flesh balloon
fritzing across your living room,
drooping against your wall.

Even the IRS declared my attention-mining
venture a casualty loss due to sudden
infestation of flying angst.

Stitches & Scars

Men never leave women unless there is another waiting.
so, I'm not wasting my love
on you any more.

I found someone younger and better
looking, a nonsmoker, who is even
more willing than you to ignore me.

??? Elu

When I stare into your alabaster face, black
eyes deep, long lashes flail my lower chakras
in silent assault, no breath streams out my mouth.
I silently invite you to reach below ember's lust,
burning cats, wail of brides on fire, dive below
your lowest rib, up behind the cage, grab a beaten
heart, rip it from sinewed moorings, press it flat
on yellow parchment, all gory gasping; you've
just written your very first Maro Markarian.

behold shawna

there is no man strong enough in mind or brawn
who can be your ever-constant friend and lover
although your pale blues, white skin, and blonde
locks draped on lithe shoulders attract able suitors,
like moths to summer's porch light, the entrance fee
measured in everlasting indentured servitude,
unrewarded by soft touches and private shares of self
foreshadowed by your reigns of absence, black hole
of reciprocity.

Combustion

You ignited my well fire.
Endless feed to burn,
I torched the night sky.

Popped off my top hat, we
shag danced in the devil's
slippers. Conflagration reigned.

Sirens beckoned toward molten coals.
We burned bedposts, asphalt off roads,
bridges to eternity.

Belladonna recaptured your body.
With as little as a changed mind,
you top-killed my well head.

Blaze out, feed plugged, like a self-cleaning
oven, what's left was a little pile of gray ash
from our drippy messes.

A bottomless pit for more arson, I'm blind
to consequence, my hands crawl low arroyos,
strike iron rocks for latent sparks.

Cowboy Jake's Lament

I'm sittin' in my underpants at Ramada of Austin,
and I'm thinkin' of you. Chewin' on a praline
from Jaime's, and feelin' poor 'n blue.

I know I'm the Rainbow Generation
but the only pot I've got is not overflowin'
doubloons. It's a hairy-belly glacier
oozin' o'r the top-of-my Fruit-o-the Looms.

I'm starin' out the window here in Austin,
and I'm thinkin' of you twice.
My dreams of us together R just a pile
on the sidewalk below, digested by lice.

You tol' me I could see you when hubby was gone,
s'long as I didn't touch. Then I gave you all the heart
I had, which you said wasn't much,
so I'm gonna get along now,
before m' jaws get too tight,
jus' like these strainin' underpants
that keep me up all night.

Dame Noir

Backyard tomato on a sizzlin' griddle,
her beret is only the first warning flasher,
cocked over straight black hair to shoulders.
Kiss-my-ruby-lips-red 6" pumps, blood pools,
yours, on shiny ink-marble floor. Armani
draped over thin bones built for hydraulics.
Old-fashioned nylons, garters, yell for a hand's
easy slide toward the center of our universe.
Seductress, homicidal with motherly love,
cruel angle of brows above an alabaster face.
Go ahead, try to snatch her to douse lust-fires,
but don't be surprised to find yourself jerking
a soda solo in a back alley off of Melrose Ave.
Because this girl goes her own way, stand back,
she'll call the shots from here on out—thank you.

All She Wrote, Long and Dry

"I'm sorry to be so late responding.
I've not yet reaccustomed myself
to closure of dangled text threads.
Been up, and occasionally down,
mostly happy, yet divorces aren't
pleasant. I just finished my first
semester at work, which brought
a feeling of accomplishment. So,
apparently I remain a bit sentient.
Although there's no time for you,
I saw A--- last night, and a week ago,
also, when C--- was in town, we met
over glasses. I still have such fond
memories of our retreat group floating
to mind, and of you and your lush
poetry, yet not enough of a fondness to
give you the time of day, or even
the common courtesy of timely replies.
Take care at a distance so as not to
perturb my narcissistic vortices."

Draga

He walked away from you, not
because of lack of care, no. Fear
of infatuation overtaking common sense,
yes, slavery to his illusions of you as
the one who completed himself
filled the void where maturity
should reside, certain that your
perfection, as sex-nurture object,
with no other mission to perform
than submission to his every whim,
would interfere with your husband's
legal rights to claim your bondage.

Fish Tale

I met a barracuda at Monterrey airport.
She flopped into the seat next to mine,
described her visit to the aquarium,
how much her kids loved to eat the other fish.
Every sentence ended with a small bubble.
I heard her teeth grind, my anus puckered.

Happy Birthday Daughter

Doc hands me the newborn; it's a girl, so that's why
her heart-rate was elevated. Bassinet, warm water,
I rinse off the placental goo. Eyes just now open, she bats
eyelashes at me, flirts. I'm a goner, that moment forward.

Plus thirty years, the ERs tell me she's dying, not their job
to save her from multiple overdoses, many months running.
Street-smart choir sings a hopeless state of mind and body.
Lonely, am I the only one who understands her fatal disease?

But Dad, I don't think I'm one of those, like you are, echoes
the deceased through thin cold lips. Leave the problem alone—
it will take care of itself, it always does past the gates of insanity
into death—plan her memorial, another victim on the way down.

I was powerless to save her soul; the mortal coil stops graveside.
Through my puddles I watched a miracle in tonight's ten-year
medallion celebration, circle of hands held by hearts not glum.
Our brothers and sisters loved her until she could love herself.

Heavy with Child

When your daughter tells you that she is pregnant,
the one you championed from the day she slid out.
That's got to be a very strange situation for you,
washed over with memory of what you
felt like when you revealed to me in our living room
that the bandage on your arm, from Cedars' doctor,
meant you were going to birth a human but you didn't
know what that meant, and neither did I. Your mother
knew, and you know now, what she felt like, all those lost
nights, terrors for the baby's survival. Wild dreams,
sorrows, roam the mindscape and your sweet little girl,
 her Mary Janes long since given to the Salvation Army,
is on the same path you were, and there's nothing
you can do about it.

How Cat Saved Our World from Germs
A sonnet

Strawberry hair, honed buck-knife tongue.
The Cat yells at poet who exits toilet,
"Did you wash your hands?" He goes back in.
I cut her some slack, but not that much.
Urine comes out sterile so what's the biggy?
OK, if I dribble a little in my pants, it stinks,
but what does that have to do with my hands?
Next time in the loo I wash my hands, 'cuz Cat.
Figure if she asks me I'll say, "Sure did.
Want to smell them?" Will only take so much
guff before I lash out my own stiletto tones.
Wherever I go now, I always wash hands
and see Cat's red lips mime that admonition.
Don't know if germ free or not, but Cat's happy.

How to Write a Confessional

Lift your tit onto a granite ledge. Grab
a loose stone with irregular edges. Focus
all your arm's strength. Smash that rock
into your naked breast. Place the sensations
on a blank page in pointed phrases.

Chug beer from brown bottles. Break
one on the edge of your birth-home's door step.
Hold the neck tightly. Scrape Dad's fetus off
your uterus. Paint the matted blood and egg
on the page, in the shape of a question mark.

Stand in a Boston classroom and kindle small glows
within poets-in-waiting. Use napalm to spread
flames into the pentameter illumination of children's
headstones. Connect your Hoover-vacuum hose
from your car's tail pipe to the driver's-side window.

Birmingham Braves

Don't you hate it when you see an old person,
realize that you went to high school together?

At my 50th Reunion, my hair grey, face tanned,
I dressed crisp like any struttin' dude on the Strip.

From the looks of it, my library-paste white
classmates stayed indoors for 50 years.

The most beautiful girl in class, then,
and now, insisted I bop with her, OK!

Fifty years ago she treated me like dog shit on a shoe,
but all the leading men in our class are dead now.

Two years after our steamy dance she crossed over
from brain cancer. A poem's in there somewhere.

For the Queen of the Pig People

I like weird people
black sheep.
eight balls.
left-of-centers.
wallflowers.
bizarros.
loners.
rejects.
outcasts. outsiders.
odd ducks.
eccentrics. The broken.
The lonely.
The lost and forgotten
I see you

Vachine

jett plain

hurt me like you are joan jett
and i am her signature guitar
flat pick my g string with vibrato
strum my heart strings at full amp
I am worthless without your wa wa

Letter to Daughter, Not Mailed

Don't ask me what to do.
I spent months in wards taking
the poisons out of my thoughts.

Now you have pressed
me to balance life again.
I knew who I was saving
in the west-wing day room.

Who am I saving now—
a grandchild, powdered
and pukey, its bobble-head

on my chest,
so my plastic heart valve
can click her to sleep?

That life was made
by you and him.
The runes are tossed.

Looks Fade, Intimacy Is Forever
For Lynn

It's always in our eyes, openness to fail,
trust in the partner's intention to support.

The role furnishes the stage but our eyes
carry our bonded connection forward.

A quick peek, a mere pass of the moment
forms no partnership. Eyes locked, pupil to pupil

through windows of the soul. That's where
all there is worth living for waits silent.

Love Poem #687

Often wrong never in doubt lips,
blonde locks fallen on no shrug
shoulders, eyes blue laser weapons,
I fell for you like the Goombah
skied straight into a Heavenly tree.

Jersey girl moxie over a kindred soul.
I saw your bright star up on the walk
of fame, your fire-hose torrent of me
messaged that I didn't make your cut.
To my credit, Sista, nor did you.

maggie's nipple shadow

maggie's nipple shadow
was the final diagnosis
our love was not toxic
avoided the drama of carcinogenic nodules
yet did not rate high on the romance scale
a mere image projection
passing flirt a brush kiss
never achieved postcoital
vaginal discharge of a
million swimmers onto
crisp percale sheets of a
summer afternoon tryst.

Marine Biology 101

She learned that sea water heals wounds faster,
so leaped into Monterrey Bay with her heartbreak,
and drowned.

Masque

When I stare into your wizened face,
through my pupated soul-windows,
the creases beside your bright eyes
sound all the laughter ever loosed;
the furrowed-field-rippled brow
chants lullabies to each sick-child
sleepless night, dimples, wracked
into shape by every broken heart,
now softer. I feel your cruise-ship
frenzy, know the feather lightness
after abandonment of desire to punish,
relish your exultation of convocation
when kids graduate from an Ivy university.
Never too late to journal cadenced verse,
evoke existential resolve to pay forward
alchemy codes, from leaves of grass to
Queen.

Bad Night for Meat

I walk into Monty's
Steakhouse. Hostess
asks if I am meeting
someone. I tell her
maybe someday. She
replies, you are in
the right place, we're
all single here. I leave.

Pervert

You bend low,
ample bosom
strains your blouse,
quietly ask my
seated face if I
am entertainment
industry member.
No, I say to your
retreating back but
am a performer, at
the same time get
why Harvey jerks off.

Metrical Feet

A woman in class showed me a poem,
how it went along a straight line, jumped
to another line. She said the line broke.
I hoped I would not have to pay for it.

She carefully explained a trochee,
I chuckled at her rapid articulation,
told her to chill the quick tempo.
I want to waltz, so bring that on.

Her need for attention a bottomless pit,
A refueling station for her hungry chasm,
I hollered for her to enjamb her own self,
slowly backed away from cadenced rhyme.

My Ex Said

"Men only want one thing"
Not me.
First I want to do it. Then,
I want to wash up. Then,
I want to leave, fast.

Northern Michigan

Sweet Alpena queen you
charlie-horsed my heart,
box-cuttered my grasp,
laughed while I bled.
You cluttered my closet
with honey-chil' smiles.
Pouty ruby red lips
pressed on an invitation
to stand at your stage door
for tricks and treats; you
lied like an evangelist
on whores. Oh baby oh
wherefore art thou when
mourning becomes Electra?

Note Found on Marilyn Monroe's Grave

Do not love me with dry syllables
pouted over your frosted lips
like indigestible tumbleweeds
rolling in parched October winds.

Pull love from your wetter places,
cul-de-sac intestines,
slick, twisted agonies
of conflicted bile, or
random pendants of blood.

Love me back when I reach inside myself,
underneath breast-plate, below pre-verbal fabric,
rip out ancient stitches across the mouths
of chamois pockets where sandbox agates click.
Loose threads, quivering in Summer sprinkles;
cheer with me over our treasures.

Porch Scene

Count on me to abandon you.
Yet, there are a few upon whom
I have never given up. My door
opens a pencil-thin crack for more,
even though I am the last house
on the block with the light on.

Recovery
For Karen Black (1939–2013)

I am homesick for a home to which I cannot return,
a home which never was; the nostalgia, the yearning,
the grief for those lost places of my past in the same way
that birds are always hungry. Thoughts best left to drift by
like puffy white clouds of a windy morning, the moist sod
on my back, meditation into a denim sky.

To entertain this domestic chasm is to set up camp outside
the gates of insanity, reach down into that damp pre-verbal
pit below the residence of heartbreak, underneath the patio
of denial, down to where the gremlin's triangular teeth flash,
where there are no sounds to represent a holler for rescue.
That container, when burst, surges like a force-five typhoon,
scale-ten earthquake, and rinses all away in tsunami's retreat.

I go there anyway, rip out the roots of Hell, eat the bitter tendrils
until drunkenness from the evil sap wobbles the legs, drives
me to my knees, into an unfamiliar dreamscape, where furry bats
flutter past my ears and on down the river; lips move in prayer
to an uninvited god. A plea for reclamation of childhood's
embrace of mother's bosom; her hums stroke my temples
with soft vibes, ease the fall into slumber's surrender.

...and Shirley Runs Esalen's Farm

Shovel in her truck for shoring berms,
cheers through tears for living rain;
sorrow for fertile soil washed to sea,
stifles flora meant for each guest's plate,
drain and gain on the littoral plain.
An earth and moon cycle, as her own,
thistle and thyme, issues of her bounty,
baked into home-kneaded black bread.
Patience for latent produce's sprouts,
long hugs doled out to recent joiners
in their fits of heartbreak to hasten
the farm's harvest yield. No agenda
other than thrive, and redolent Spring
lowers sprinkled 'round, beacons
for buzzy pollinators above forever
swells that roll on. And on.

Garrison Station

No more passenger trains for this stop,
architecture rarely seen anymore, glazed
brick box in a town the same size, distant
from rough edges of the city grass between
its tracks, humidity taken its due from the
tarnished rails, creosote cross-ties greyed,
leaning trackside water tower detached spout,
tank drained, once a week freight rolls on down
the spur line, flashes red caboose, blind.
Only silence of the lunar surface left within
the empty vessel now so dry its bottom
a home to a cold-blooded horned toads.
Abandoned, as though the tiny cube caught
mental illness, homeless through no fault
of its own, shunned like a scarlet letter, the sin
of age unpardonable for longer than eternity,
missing three red clay roof tiles, the gap cries out
like a three-year-old separated from her mother
in the Walmart dry goods row.

Those Things You Don't Do

Everyone needs a little time away — CHICAGO

I've enjoyed mine from you so much
I decided to make it permanent.
Because, when we were together
I expected you to do things that,
when you didn't, made me mad.

That wouldn't be so bad
if you purposely withheld those things.
But, I now know you don't even have
those things.

Which still makes me mad.
But, without you around
it passes rather than festers.

Now you're gone, and so are they.

two cents change

stood next to me her
hand on my arm said
i love you you do know
that don't you i said
well yes you keep telling
me but what about the nazi
official's phrase that a lie
repeated often and loud
enough will be believed
i lit my last camel she said
you jews are so full of self
hatred you visit auschwitz
like it was a resort she slinked
into the parking lot sang
"hold my hand it's a long way
down to the bottom of the river"
i rubbed the revolver in my jacket
pocket fingered the little trigger
why am i your enemy i do not restrain
your forward trajectory put my foot
in your door invade your neuroses i
am not a male chauvinist pig my mother
never knew the glass ceiling she rose
above barnyard chatter ran her brother's
bookstore after his sentence to the
penitentiary buy-low sell-high the rest
fell into the bank how did i become your
punching bag i never groped you bitched
you is it the mere fact of my plumbing
are you able to detect the amped infrared
intensity of my testes my imperative to

pump swimmers into your orifices are
you offended that when i'm with you i
can't find my car, that when i want to
converse all that comes out are plosives
and glottals are you rueful that you don't
have your own dick what causes the
incoming male-bash mortars epithets
such as my only worth is upper-body
strength and sperm my love for you is like
a barge full, up on the hudson pushed by
a rusty tug exposed cargo of rock candy
softened by your squalls of whim
turbine blades thrust against currents
silent below the water-line opposing
our nuptial feast i turn, stare at you
asleep on our bed curled body beneath
the sheets feral like a fox sweat mats
your flaxen hair your ripeness a
reminder of how hard I love you
every day you awaken a cause for my
celebration certain we will be so until
the winds whisk our ashes asunder i feel
so helpless to return the attention
you've given me needing to be inside of
you, yet knowing if I walk across
the suite stroke your hip sirens will set my
vessel adrift to the mercies of tidal flood
and eddytrap pools gather in my eyes i
wait for rescue i wouldn't know then
that you saw my generosity as folding
money on a whore's bed that the next
monday you killed yourself.

Yama

A new light bathes my torso, nimble gentle fingers caress my limbs,
coos as soft as a turtle dove's breast fill places I forgot were empty.
Lips the nutty flavor of sweet cream and bitter tea in the morning, her
face a Weather Channel report on the climate along destiny's high-way.
A hippie at core, hair dye masks those silver strands that blow her cover,
God damn, have I fallen in love? A reservist called out to serve again?

Polly Vocal's All Girl Band

Debbie said, "Too soon after Clem's death
for us to shack up"; Ronda said, "I always
ask you out to dinner, you never ask me."
My therapist said they weren't available.
Hey, I gave them many chances to get
available but something in their past must've
made it impossible for them to love me
in the way I need to be loved—accepted
is a better word or maybe it's because
I met them all in AA meetings. All I ask
is, hear me, laugh with me—not at me.
Dance with me, this guy who only knows
how to sway gently with slow music,
our bodies held close, pace tiny circles
that always go nowhere.

Pathways

Mother morning glorys Esalen, absorbs rays of sol.
Dancers in Fritz's dim living room sway, punctuate
with hip, elbow, syncopated knee dips—easy pick-up
chorus line. I don't belong here. Need a new workshop
added to her catalogue. Just sit in a sunny garden chair,
an Adirondack wholly made of Trex, loud explosions of poppy
blossoms, frigid freshet off white caps in the bay gales over blue
kale rows, chills my chest below poetry-book-in-hands. I turn
for warmth to a bath of sunshine no-work-no-shop seminar.
Mama-baby bump strolls by sez hey, me right back at 'er. Daddy
made that mama-baby bump, mama made that mama-baby bump
in the night, baby on board swims with purpose above the dusty
foot-worn trail. Hard Times Require Furious Dancing. Alice Walker's
tome throws down African. "I was born to grow, alongside my garden plants,
poems like this one," not in a dungeon where prancers stub toes on stones
along intimacy's trail.

About Times

I lost my cream of tomato
colored watch today in
TSA's security tunnel.

Rushed to unbuckle
the offending object
with the same immediacy
I fumbled to launch the rage
between my legs on its
first conquest at seventeen.

Although she had not resisted
surrender of our virginity, she
impatiently chewed gum
for arrival at third base.

Skirball Reading Elevator Chat

She: Are you a poet too? Are you also a painter?
Me: Oh, I painted a house one time.
She: Is that a poem?
Me: No. I used a brush and a bucket.
She: It's a better poem.
I thought, I didn't want to paint, or talk either.
But, if she was nice to me, I would marry her,
wait for illusion's dash on the rocks before
the bailout.

Bucky & Flo

We open a door to where there is no road, we take it.
—Philomene Long, from poem *Marriage*

A pheromone ceremony washed off by shell casings
and postcard platitudes, cover up Flo's belt buckle
scars under Dreads of a Project's upbringing
in the circus town of angels and trapeze whores,
swingers of shuffles and jive. Bucky's knuckles,
raw from the 'Hood holds Flo's hand 'cross the low
stone bridge named Trust under which elephants
escape from the couple's living room to die
in the jeweler's ring. No one's the wiser 'cept
street cats be bopin', knee droppin', skirt twirlin'
shag dancers of a Saturday drag a doob home
wedding, vows worth only so much as the tats
they're written on. Mother disappeared
into Terminal Island prison. Uncle Joe took
over from rover, slipped a bone of his own,
felonious assault says the judge, but it's better
than being alone. Together Bucky and Flo loosen
the nooses of ancient trauma, thrive on the Now.
Blues 'monica, washtub base on Venice Boardwalk.
Sunday parade of Crackers and Rednecks, drawl
the only difference, Pramsters, Gangsters mix too,
all toss bread in the hat and moooo on.

Prayer

Breakups require wild writing into the early hours,
attempts to capture the voices of roads not taken,
louder now that probabilities have diminished.

Coulda woulda shoulda saves a sleeping berth
on the Vortex Flyer departing from ground zero.
Last stop, the mournful gates of Insanity and Death.

Toss the shredded rags of trust into the bucket list,
keep doin' whatcha doin' gonna keep on gettin'
whacha gettin'. Weathaman turn that sky blue.

Highland Park Film Festival

Racatacata beats on North Figueroa store fronts.
Tight skirts and wife beaters salsa as in a velvet
painting of naked dancers, their bulges pouted.
The kind you buy in Tijuana, and hide from your wife
until she finds it in the garage. You tell her it was left
there, behind the folded card table, by a Homeless.

Her resentment simmers slowly like a frog
in sauce pan water doesn't notice temperature
rising until it's too late to jump. Until she feels
her mortgage threatened by your lying eyes
and either bolts to her mother's house in Norwalk,
or beds the pool guy on Monday morning.

And you forgive her truancy not because of anger
management or AA but because when you look into
each other's eyes the memories of fetuses passed,
repaired credit reports, and a tiny vegetable garden
tended as partners reside on the summit of vows
made in that bright May marriage of bloods.

Song for Wrinkles

After the reading one of them said, "The poem
is about a woman's lost beauty." You mean
to tell me that a mother's placental push,
her bedside vigil with baby's colicky night,
hubby's affairs, another lost fetus of a baby
who couldn't stay, a Harvard degree, a GED,
a bar-fight lost, a bar-fight won, crossing
Jordan of more loves than can be counted.
—all things known to cause wrinkles are
ugly metrics of lost beauty? What about
a vinyl record, each wrinkle resonates a tune
against all odds, sets the toes to tapping,
a dance backwards in heels that hasn't ended, yet.
Who else will hold daughter's hand when her
period first arrives and say, "Sweetie, let's celebrate,
go for coffee and the best chocolate we can find,"
who else can read the Marine Corps letter
"Corporal Malone was killed in an urban firefight
in Fallujah", open her mouth and just say his name,
"Johnny!", who else can labor morning and afternoon
composing Sunday supper and have cheer to say,
"Come and get it!" That's the song that platter spins,
hallelujah, hallelujah, hallelujah.

Hurry Up Sailor

I have never used a whore. I'm told there is a sense
of urgency to get off, Johns-per-hour the key metric
of productivity. Not unlike a poetry workshop,

where a short pithy poem with a punch line, a strong close,
is expected. Brevity is embraced so that all the budding poets
turn a quick trick or receive a severe tongue lashing.

Focused readings prompt excessive remarks like
"I loved the penultimate line, I loved the last stanza,
I loved the rogue ambiance." Alphanumerically more love
than any fornications with a woman of the night, and, as
with Chinese food, hungry again after thirty minutes.

Lies

Obscure sentences skulk
in a forsaken corner.

Yellow keyhole eyes, like lines
of highlighter on black velvet.

Cloaked haunches perched
on the peaks of closet shadows.

Plots spun in darkness' clutter
gather speed on the way back.

Paradigms rattle the panes of habit,
an auditor's coin taps the front door.

Job Description

Mothers and their gender
hover with multi-sensors.
Drones with rhinestones
keep babies safe,
welcome them home
from the hunter's hill.
Bleed in places
there are no wounds.
Chop wood, carry water,
repeat, sweat, repeat.

Muse

W. S. Merwin's Muse is not lazy
like mine. Shows up daily,
not just for the High Holy Days

Garden hose streams a brook
of crystal dots on Summer dry soil
where no sprouts grow
yet. I am

certain that my water work
produces stalks of corn,
green, with yellow kernels
named after me.

Beneath ear silk
Mr. Worm eats row upon
row of tasty niblets.
I am full.

Yet I am
named after me.
I am full.

Power Animal

"You are Puma," chanted my Shaman,
shawled in a little room. Sage
smoldered in a cobalt bowl.
I've not prowled the undergrowth
since Emphysema took her.

Vachine

Requiem for a Black Sea Sturgeon

Hooked beluga found so hard ecstasy escaped
her lips in Romanian. Days later her body
floated up on the beach with the high tide.
Gulls the only witnesses to her expiration
in the austerity of seaweed odors and sand,
without a gathered school of mourners.
She always wanted her final flops to be high
drama but at the end she just silently returned
to our Mother with the receded backwash.

Sabbath Observed

Electric menorah branches topped
by filaments flickered orange flames.
Pretend candles lit by a virtual woman.
Timed for Fridays at sundown. Cheer Jews'
safety in living rooms, brothers, sisters,
parents too. Children fed, swaddled,
"Goodnight noises everywhere."

Sacred Space
For Flowers

Sun rays filter through eucalyptus branches
pattern the mottled roadway approach from
opposite directions Baby Mercedes scant room
for one meet in mutual recognition halt window
to window slide open to booms of sea on cliffs
unseen known only by thunder on loose topsoil
and tires hands wrists arms reach for the clasp
rooted in their deepest chakras souls dance
to strains of meta-music earth shifts axis spins
around woman man in their tango of past toils
now becalmed in the instant eyes meet pupil
to pupil returned to the orchard before the apple
naked without blush.

Shadow Players

Roses are bled
Violence, code blue.
Da Judge done laid down a TRO
especially at you.

Stranger

I think She is the Me I think I am. But, since I don't know who I am, she always ends up being a stranger.

Billy Wilder said it better, "Her marriages didn't work out because Joe DiMaggio found out she was Marilyn Monroe, and Arthur Miller found out she wasn't Marilyn Monroe."

Stuffed Animal

The smiley bride-to-be, nuptial skirt butt-crack-tight,
high hemmed thighs bulged to her knees, our first meeting.
Through cracking gum, she shouted to my new girlfriend
"He's a Teddy bear." Her big-haired posse cackled approval.

On a steep sandy beach, the cusp of Hanalei Bay,
the couple's marriage vows, mumbled through sunset
surf and open sea gusts, raise the headwinds of my
axe-murderer temper and withheld inner child

that blew my exes to divorce. Unlike the groom,
I have no criminal convictions or temporary restraining
orders, no court-directed anger management classes.
Girls may adore Teddy, but they marry felons.

Union Station Ticket Agent

Juanita O'Brien, brass name tag
lacquered black letters, bottom chipped
off the A, pinned on her jazz-blue tunic,
nugget of sleep cornered
in one doe-eye.

Her man, Jimmy, laid track for awhile,
drank tanks of brew before he flopped,
one Spring night in an outskirt of Barstow,
where she found him, under her trailer windowsill,
loose boots snoring in morning glories.

Between his jig and her lagrimas
the couple had enough time together
to whelp Mable and Flo
before he and his bucket of stale starts
fumed back out on the rails.

Tonight, as Juanita sweeps
change from the cash drawer
Super Chief wails Jimmy's serenade,
a late arrival at Track 2 after issues
with a big rig in Rialto.

Introvert

My psychotherapist told me that I have a need
for close association with other humans as though
I were one of them. That's why I go to parties,
even though my intestines are in spasm.

I always wear the black T-shirt with white letters
that spell "Go Away," yet still attract social pollen
gatherers, like bees in bloom season, who probe
my face with where-you-from-what-do-you do,
then dart to other stamens before I answer.

The doctor told me I have low self-esteem. No,
I have chronic self-hatred. I need ten more years
of therapy just to get to self-esteem issues.

Doc told me I lack empathy. I took lessons, learned
to ask open-ended questions, seek more response
than just a yes, or a no. I asked even more questions
about, what do you call them, their feeling words.
I still do not give a tinker's damn about their answers.

Be Right Back

Last night the great full moon of April,
next one in nineteen years, when it's expected
I'll be passed over River Jordan, but death
is over-rated, in fact does not exist.

I was not born. I have always been alive.
When my vessel becomes worn out,
my gems will return to their source, shine
again somewhere in our star-stuff landscape.

I attempt to pay love forward, as is the advice
of those who study such things—Moses is one.
Yet as I near the sunset, still there are claw
marks on my offerings.

I do not dread death. That my body fearfully
seeks to protect itself, a mere consequence
of my animal manifestation. No angst either
over loss of my beloveds, won't be abandoned.

I'll always be a breeze in their mind-wind,
dance in the Sabbath candle's flicker.
Tread gently on our blue-green planet,
it's me upon whom you will be walking.

Winter Solstice at Esalen, Big Sur

Ocean booms below the Lodge, odd poets
gather like butterflies. Dazzling sunlight
coaxes scent from fir-trees we inhale
until intoxicated by Christ's molecules

Seekers in Big Yurt, perched upon pillows,
await turns to read hastily scribed yearnings
from lap-journals, as day swifts into darkness.

We rejoice day's end, ease into the velvet pocket
of the long, long night, Midnight sky so clear
our Milky Way lights the foot-worn garden path.

A thin clearing across six-score acres of black soil
gulched by a rapid rivulet. We sip from an eddy
of the little river until we too become loud water.

Seminal hot-springs course into stone baths soothing
sinew and bone since the Indigenous. Earth's own fire
heats the liquid so hot we return to our molten core.

I stare at a poet's nakedness. She stares back.
I become another bright shiny bead on the string
wrapped 'round her ring-finger. We meet in bed.

Lips, tongues, fingertips travel long strokes, discover
spots where crowdlets of throat sounds mingle above
our limbs' thicket. A bomb-burst of morning sun burns
off fog by afternoon.

The shine shimmies the bay. Forever sea sounds, and a rare
neap tide, beckon writers inside the dim hall, draw a choir
of poetry from our loins. Loneliness lifts like a gauze blanket.

Samson

Samson died that afternoon,
ball took a wild bounce from
our porch, into the empty
street, auto barreled along,
struck him midair. Quick
trip to the vet, who shook
his head slowly, shoved
a blade between my ribs.
Oh, distraction avoids those
constant jack-knifed curls
on my floor, agonal rage
still behind draped shadows.

Pre

My doctor told me I was pre-diabetic, but
isn't that like pre-death,
I don't have diabetes yet.

Getting on an airplane is called boarding, but
when the announcement to pre-board is made
why are people getting on? Isn't that boarding?

Premonition means forewarning, but
If I'm worried about the event to be
isn't it like it's already happened?

Prejudice is conclusion before facts, but
If a tree falls in a wilderness forest
is the husband still wrong?

Pre-intercourse is called foreplay, but
when the golfer says "Fore" isn't that
a shouted warning of physical danger?

A prior-to-marriage contract is a pre-nuptial, but
If I don't trust that woman,
why am I marrying her?

Marriage Sonnet

So excited about my upcoming wedding with myself.
Same as my friend who aisle-walked her gown solo
after the to-be partner awakened and remembered he
was self-sufficient. After all, I'm the best pal I've got.
No more emptiness on Valentine's Day or New Year's.
Hip, slick, and cool. Smoother than the Glide Choir, yo.
New tux jacket, white Gardenia, no pants. Just a jockstrap
and spats, 'cuz why not? Small intimate venue, say a Forest
Ranger's tower. Witnesses toss rice pudding, no caterers.
Without a reception either because Facebook Goings don't.
No Rabbi'll take this gig so it's Eddie Izzard, in dinosaur drag.
Don't want any Evangelist pickets outside since it's same sex.
Wedding night problematic, I mean, I don't want to go blind.

mama said

your eyelids droop you
look like a chink
sometimes i wonder
who your father is
not that guy
i married gone to war
god only knows where
she cried I touched her hand
said ma it gon be ok
i am right here
it gon be fine
juz you wait n see
allz well what ends
next mornin in school
i made a plaster handprint
for mother's day

Latchkey

There's nobody home
but a sofa and window
nobody to say I believe
in you no one to tell why
there's dried-blood nose'n
shirt torn below the collar
I daydream that the girl
from Encino smiled at me
a sobo lives south
of the boulevard distant
not someone I ever talk
to she doesn't see nobos
who live on the Valley floor
with toxic runoff croaking toads
at seventeen there is no place
for my hands I watch a ford
commercial see what the
passenger does with his hands
how do you say hi how
are you would you like
to see a movie just
the two of us she summers

in dip the toes st tropez
knows why dupars puts a pat
of butter on their burger bun
dines at the rams horn where dad
said the host lips are so tight
he must have a rubber band round
his asshole she never rides the bus
on ventura from hayvenhurst
to noble in ghetto sherman oaks
a plane from the airport two blocks
over roars overhead a jet fighter
so loud the dream turns to nightmare
she will marry captain of the swim team
who'll dumb luck into investment banking
my dad is at work has heart attacks, ulcers
my mom works with skin rash won't go away
her migraines all weekend girl-from-encino
swimmer-man will die prematurely leaving her
only social skills and a son who'll try to pay
tuition writing songs sung in odor stained
coffeehouses there's nobody's home.

Vachine

> "I felt seen for the first time, because I had let myself be seen." —Jewel

abuse shows in her tight eyes
beatings isolation starved warmth
embrace fears of their long tongues
in her throat moved often suspect of
changes in her living quarters broken
sidewalks rape stares of passers-by
pets her hair not to feel so all alone
who will save your soul carries freight
of the unexamined life rejected and
scores a full scholarship for honesty
filled with great art go away and listen
voices below the depression of a cheap
motel in havasupai lead to the river cold
from hibernation below the dam cots
under cottonwoods sufficient sustenance
of slumber to sing agates from canyon haze

Bleeding Deacon for the Afflicted

Thanksgiving, gratitude, is the gospel
preached in the Church of Shit Happens,
where it's taught to hug yourself Divine
in the still of nighttime called loneliness.

Solo, no one else in sight, without a knot
in the rope on which to brake the decent,
an abandoned child's screech for mother
only one section over in their grocery market.

"Why me" wastes ego, Bigger than oneself.
Shit doesn't even know you, just the crack
of a whip, What Goes Around Comes Around
and It Picks Up Speed On the Way Back.

Vachine

"The Smallest Caskets Are the Heaviest"
—Ernest Hemingway

Nobody can explain why a child
has to die, certainly G-d does not
kill children, does she? Or do you
mean to tell me that G-d drowned
that Syrian boy washed up on the beach?
That his parents were rendered powerless
to fend off water's obstruction of the
justice of air. Is that what I'm supposed
to believe? I don't care whose god
you choose, they just don't end
lives of the young. Lucille Clifton
planned to ask her god to explain
the deaths of her two children
because she was pissed they were
taken from her arms. Yet I pray
for a reason for the death of our
unborn first child, why mother's job
description was tossed into that dumpster
along with our fetus. Dagger my chest

so I feel what mother felt, drain my eyes
into salt flats, deliver me the imperative
to surrender my life. Place a sorrow wafer
onto this tongue so I can whisper grief
into my wife's ear. Infuse in me a deity's
tolerance when she has not even set water
out for supper yet, long into recovery.
She cross-stitches by gold-dusted twilight,
past the cusp of Summer. Second-boy breathes
slumber-songs next to her on the covered
weather porch. Conestoga heritage of
the endless prairie tugs her breastbone.
Door County memories drift into Season's-end
breeze. First-boy, hand-in-hand with Steve,
his grandfather in plaid, rustle tinder-stalks
of backyard cornfield. Drop a stitch at dusk,
loop back for soul retrieval, lantern dims
for all the babies who couldn't stay.

Where Does the Laughter of Children Go?

Say Boo Boo Butt in a class of second graders,
hear a riot of sides splitting, the roar of abandon
to raucous bliss without regard to threats of safety.
A chorus of kinder racket lifting the surroundings.

Does it sink under the horizon early like Equinox,
to surface ever so slowly afterward during Solstice?
Must chimes of joy be bidden rise by a Druid princess
eager to party down on the sod of Stonehenge's circle?

What so terrifies youngsters that they clam up as adults?
Where do fire-spewing dragons lurk in their psyches?
Which circuit breaker gets tripped so their responses
to gibberish become flat affect and avoidance of the mirth?

Does the rap of mother's knuckles on a young face
so stifle further ha has that the child's assessed well being
burrows underground like a furtive gopher, whiskers
twitching to find the right sanctuary in which to tunnel?

Awaken your child's roar of glee, act stupid for once.
Talk in tongues until youngsters pee pants unable
to harness the meandering path of their funny bones.
Guffaw from the gut like life depended—'cuz it does.

Denouement

When I looked around you had slipped away
on Sunday morning, sad I couldn't say 'bye.
Didn't know you had other demands, miles
to go before you slept, a race to horizon
with a sun's trajectory of your own to follow.
Held my breath every time you spoke during
our time because each thing you said was so
poetic—carefully chosen words said slowly.
How empty I felt when your scent in our yurt
was absent, only silence, no defense against
itself. I was a good wife and mother those years,
my vessel now drains faster than refilled, bones
visible where muscle was before, a void
not visited by sustenance.

Mercy

I caught my fish limit
in the shadow of
Petaluma's counterweight
drawbridge.
Two pink salmon way off
their route to the
Columbia ladders.
Lopped off one's head
fed to my cat who sucked
the bones clean,
looked at me like I had
felonied her.
If this cat was much larger
she would eat me. No
interrogatories, no depositions
Her incisors into my throat
the way a lioness downs
a gazelle by the neck first,
punctures the jugular,
calls in cubs
to work over the entrails,
only the hard carcass remains,
like my Marital Property
Settlement in and for
the County of Sonoma, CA.
Drawbridge rises, frees
the channel for boat traffic again.
While still gasping and wriggling
I release the other salmon
back into the river with Godspeed
to San Pablo Bay.

PART IV
SELECTED POEMS

"I'd rather write about polar bears than people."

—Mary Oliver

Of Places

Lost and Found
For Sierra

Rare I walk on the beach under my apartment balcony.
This morning's tide left the Bay's rejects stranded, dry.
First sight looked like a dead baby octopus, on its back,
rigid core, tentacles spread like wagon-wheel spokes,
flies had not yet congregated. My fingers dug deep
in the sand, scooped up this child, laid her back down
in the backwash; she contracted, squirted ink, pulsed
toward roiled shore-break to grow old.

Ms. Blizzard

So what if storm officials closed Interstate 40
all day Wednesday?
Don't blame me.
Hey, that's the way I am.

Some travelers abandoned their autos, walked
on loud powder from Albuquerque
to Santa Rosa. I tried to turn them into popsicles,
dash their dreams of crackling Christmas hearths.

From Bernalillo to Las Vegas, N.M.,
jack-knifed big-rigs closed all major highways.
Let the good times roll.
What's the matter? Can't take a little ice?

At midnight, I draped sloppy cotton balls
on gabled condos in AngelFire.
Cowered in the little units, skiers galvanize
windowpanes with their sighs.

The kids' wails for redemption are drowned
by my turbo-gusts. When I push drifts
over their balconies, even the men cry.
Moms just gaze over choked Highway 50.

Never mind the county plow's pace,
I blow puff-laden fir branches.
They launch their overloads onto the roadbed,
filling in where the Sno-Cats just treaded.

Human beings' plights trigger my hollow howl
of yearning for the one I haven't found yet,
Mister Blizzard. You know, settle down,
whistle up your own brood.

Incompressible

Midnight ice sheets born on a former lake bed,
break up as temperatures warm, wind kicks up,
blows fragmented ice shards across the surface,
nudge bread-basket-sized rocks hard enough to move
them millimeter by millimeter. Such has been my
love for you, inevitably slow momentum over eons.

Monsoon, Phoenix

What else follows this 108-degree day?
Thunderstorms from a lazy front blown
over from Sea of Cortez' hot fornix.
Wind shrieks through our sliding door
like a Northeaster off Narragansett
in February, except it's 101 at 11 p.m.
Lightening splits a burnt-sienna horizon,
baby wakes with sounds that curdle milk—
so much for this night's shaky slumber.

Summer Solstice Indigo

So now each day is shorter, a tiny grief of lost light.
I want to sing a Christmas carol after which the days
get longer, each a tiny celebration of Sol's life-gift.
Rudolph's the only song for me 'cuz his brightness
is a 24/7 constant, and he don't cotton to solstice shit.

Nature's Game

Summer showers on Aspen.
Leaden cells pass low over
Roaring Fork Valley, silver s
quadrons drop loads, chase
villagers into bistros they
usually don't choose, soak
E. Bauer shirts on sidewalk l
overs, blow to Maroon Bells,
unleash blue bolts, thunder-claps.
Park rangers gasp over births
of multiple brush-fire pockets,
alpenglow with malice. Storm
boils on toward Pueblo-town's
desert-scape, surrenders to sand.

This Mallorca

Fieldstone walls embrace golden sands;
incense wafts from Africa's shore, fuel
for tapped shoes of Moorish flame.

Twirled wrists of olive maidens, wooed
by chants from tunicked swains,
who stand 'neath vine-grown balconies.

Chapel cistern bathe in Jesus' light.
Suitors spill honeyed promises like hot
tea lapped in haste over rigid lips.

cormorant

floats in our cove, spies motion
in the depths, bullets under glassy
surface, bogarts prey, launches above
the water line, banks a hard right onto
her perch, savors a marine breakfast,
unaware of my smoked salmon repast.

Oh, Sweet Mother of Christ,

there are spiders in Australia
who eat snakes, braggarts, not
satisfied with a tasty fly, or
ant, these buggers have long
skinny legs, like cranes, hold
a snake captive while they
chew little bites off until
there's nothing left. They're
everywhere, unavoidable,
commonplace in the iso-
lated subcontinent of Auzzies.
Tell you what—fuck that,
I'm staying in Santa Monica.

Rountree Lane Workshop

Inmates in uniforms the color of sky they can't see.
First names only, my first poetry lesson for them
begins with Bukowski, syntax of the brutal closer
to their own. Distrust on each face sourced in
ancient trauma, belt buckled, drunken punches.
No matter, I tell them all will be published poets at
workshop's end. That look at me, frozen chops
mask oceans of disappointment told in wraps.
Poet calls self Young Pak, cops to his sheet, life
outside interrupted his own fault, unlike others'
arguments on technicalities. All poems in Hallmark
rhyme, chapbook-bound distributed to their families.
Go home triple doors released horizon to horizon
puffers only for the free to roam.

What Our Moon Believes

Blessed by radiance from afar
acned Luna swings its bitch
through the space-time thing,
teaser of Earth's clitoral tides,
coitus reservatus ala maximus,
hidden dark side all the wiser.

Inconvenient Truths

Rainy Day

Walk dog
Spank monkey
Take nap

Vachine

Dark Think

Embrace the dwell that lights
the darkness, even though
in the Valley of the Shadow
of Death beware of thy rod
and thy selfie, there is no
comfort in tight Jockeys

Creed

Fuck, sustain, die—
the only purpose
of being. Everything
else indicates idle time.

About Time

Tick-tock is louder
On approach to that pine box
And speed of light slows

Au Bon Pain

If you wonder
why I don't hug you,
it's your crust.

Landay for Medusa

An aspiration of sailors' moan—
guardian of poems, her serpents' venom turns them to stone.

Landay for Skater

around her rink glides the spangled queen;
all worries fly off her furrowed brow, all signal lights green

Tangy Tercets

Marriage

Hematoma and Edema gathered
at the quay for embarkation on
their nuptial Caribbean bruise.

Protect This Child

How does Coach look into the showers,
see an adult raping a 10-year-old boy,
and not grab a baseball bat?

Window

Frozen skivvies on a clothesline,
button fly winks like the moon
held by morning's sapphire sky.

On the Rocks

If I fall for the crap
in your siren song,
I deserve bondage.

1926

Back in the day, a woman called tart
to her face could take the compliment,
return a wry smile; now it's a felony.

Part V
THANATOS

"We have art in order not to die of the truth."

—Friedrich Nietzsche

Poem Appropriated
—After Pablo, Fernando, Africa

My child is an artist.
My problem has been
how to remain an artist
once I grew up.

When this old man dies
my library will burn.
Music of my flames
will heal your soul.

Last Dream

A rusty man on a skinny bicycle
pedals toward the top of a dirt road,
trouser leg torn at the knee,
and no shoe on his left foot.

The front wheel splinters a small stone,
throws a shard up, punctures his big toe.
A black blood drop plops onto the dirt
in the shape of a screaming skull

with wide eye sockets. A granite tongue
wags an invitation, "Discover eternity
within my moribund pupils."
Coherence fades.

A magician's waxed paper
cape draws across each eye,
glass-like and unfocused,
cloaks soul's flight.

Mortician

He always gets the suicide swan-diver,
whose head Jackson Pollacks on the sidewalk.

Pieces won't fit neatly in a vinyl body bag.
Only muddled chunks, spooned from a cranial tray.

Lucky if he gets a few straight bones to reshape
jumper's final smile.

Cutting room overhead-fan the only sound;
formaldehyde hangs like a rubber sheet.

No need to boost the house lights,
the stiff is on the dark side of the road.

Mortician crosses himself, presses a scalpel along a Y-incision
from the corpse's shoulders to pubis,

sighs in the syntax of nails when organ stew hemorrhages
a purple brook to the floor drain.

Coffee pot in the corner snarls for holy water.
Cup of joe in hand, slouched in shadows against a locker,
he flasks gin to lips, chases with a pull from the mug.
A slow shrug, one tear marks him.

Lance

leans on the ground-floor elevator door post,
a Van Cleef & Arpels condo-hotel in Aspen,
pale head down. His runes tossed by Upstairs
Committee. Draws on a Camel, fills a collapsed
lung, relief on the way. So cold-wet the glowed
tip describes a 90 degree ark fueled by shivers.
Scabs raw-red opened by struggles to crawl up from
the creek where he was dumped by two-percenters
who gave at the office. Tire-iron internal bleeding.
Claw-hammer contusions sting in the sparse noon
shade. Animal control nets, kennels him in solitary,
friendless & dangerous on the APB.

read some poems at your link

heavy shit man i aspire to write
from the place you do but last time
i tried they said my piece was self-
destructive ideation not a poem
nietzsche 'sez we have art so as not
to die from the truth i first learned i was
a poet when the suicide note i hung on
your refrigerator rhymed as you read it to me
you said my death would only hurt those
closest to me but how will i know stand back
 while i return the arming pin to the grenade
that looks like a tiny pineapple in my kitchen
fruit bowl listen to me when i say that i am
homesick for where i already am that it's not
one thing after another, it's the same old thing
over and over let me explain why everyone
will be better off when I'm not here anymore
yes, you are probably right i have responsibilities
chief among which is the pursuit of happiness
but all I know is that shit is fucked up and stuff

Part VI

THE REMAINS

*"If you haven't been there,
you don't have anything to say."*

—Anonymous

Route 68 Ballet

At the hotel balcony I lean into my daydream,
awakened by crunch sounds from asphalt, a Beemer
careens into the lane of opposite traffic empty
of oncoming cars. The tangled silver machine
spews steam into the passenger compartment,
surrounds the sleek body, coils into the sky.

Button-down Beemer walks slowly toward
his rear-ended victim. Both hobble toward
a share of contact info. Injured man wobbles,
holds his back, paramedics arrive, check vitals,
walk the claimant into the EM coach, siren away.

Firemen arrive, insistent red lights, horns clear
the roadway, divert traffic, sweep debris, neon-
striped overcoats and knee-high boots command
lust in wide eyes of idle onlookers Wreakers
haul wounded steel gladiators to their bone yard.

Cops enter stage right, cruiser's party hats paint
the scene. Only the perp remains on non-stop
cell chant since inception of the post-collision
ballet. Traffic news announces injury accident
Highway 68 at Olmstead, use alternate routes,
Carmel Valley Road. Now I can't find my keys.

Rountree Lane Sunset

I see you
inmates in the yard
admire my sky
tight groups, necks craned
shoulders almost touch
walls block flamed horizon
only wire covers your ceiling
just enough Creator's light
fills your cups of yearn
no one revoked joy
I hear your praise
You are seen.

Industrial Poetry

Plenum wrench under the shim nozzle
I rammed the manual detent with alacrity,
only to discover that the gasket shank
had drifted away before false dawn.

Bushing flanged, I tried to ratchet-knurl
a bigger Yankee screwdriver and for my effort
was rewarded with oiled scupper seeds,
flummoxed out of my gourd,

I loosed a mighty pelican hook from boson's locker
and lathed the next hawse pipe to within an inch
of its choker cable, not forgetting
to vise-grip the torque nuts until ball peen squirmed.

Don't ever say that I need a metric hammer
for better results, or that an oscillating saw trumps
a reverse star bit, because I know when my
Johnson rod is arcing.

How to Write Poetry

"Never use adjectives unless you are trying to describe something and don't want to do it the hard way."
—Rick Lupert, poet

Stump Blood Axe
Sherriff Warrant Bail Trial
Dungarees

Ambition

Poetry as an occupation
has no way to make a living
by its practice.

"Hobby" seems too trite;
"Profession" has more syllables
than can be clothed and fed.

My lifetime Poet earnings—not
enough for a wholesome meal
at most local sustenance emporia.

A baby-back verb, a turnover phrase,
a bite of irony—
all that can be swallowed.

A Child of My Own

I'm your guy in the crisis of a car wreck.
My vitals do not elevate; I act out all those
rational steps they recommend in books,
an EMT on a meditation diet; depend on me
to pull our child from the flames, lift the car
off your chest. It's the same sentience when
I smell rain coming in the silence of evening's
cloud-cover and know every little thing for as far
as you can mark is in perfect balance.

from Zohar

As morning is about to lighten, light darkens
and blackens, blackness prevails.

Then a woman unites with her husband,
conversing with him, entering his palace.

Later, when the sun is about to set,
it brightens, then night comes and swallows it.

When all gates are closed, dogs bark,
donkeys tremble,

Buddha Bekins

"We are all interconnected."
—Thích Nhât Hanh

When a loved one dies, it feels like someone tore a hole in your torso, but that's just the decedent moving to a new neighborhood in our Universe.

Shattered
After the seminar "C.G. Jung and the Kabbalah"

Mend what's broken even though parts of the cup slip
through cracks in the floorboards and hide under the house
in crannies of dim soil.

Glue the vessel back together, not knowing that chips
around the shard edges are lost, so even if the pieces
are all reattached, there will be bare spots on the lip.

Guzzle deeply from that patched and tattered crockery
as though the presidential election's outcome depends
on each thirsty gulp.

Celebrate the liquid's gullet-rush,
cheer a smiling shiver's ascension
from soles to crown.

High Society

Manor house hall, the Mingles in polite circles
pose for a portrait called Smug. Girl rolls in
like a Studebaker on a Lexus showroom floor,
taffeta gown floating above standard issue combat
boots. Noses turn skyward for a scent of familial
feces. Even the limp-wrist crowd looks down,
but the chatter goes on, not a syllable dropped,
because, after all, they know who they are,
and she isn't. Conversations of country clubs,
Yale tuition for the buns, no mention of that hussy
in the foyer, crimson scarf clashing with purple
bodice louder than a criminal's empty protests
of incursions against greed. Beneath all underwear
compressed kinky hair all indistinguishable.

Gibberish

Tiger swoon snipe hunt jackalope scope.
moon dog poon tang spread eagled dope.

Nope, piss up a rope, say you're the Pope.
Hairy chest glacier breaks beyond cope.

Claire de Lune zoom crotch belly launch.
Cheese dip honey sip suckle under paunch.

Helm to lee ducka da boom too soon bang.
Genny luff sheets windage gust rook hang.

Missing baby wolf pack makes a point.
Buzz free smart car blows this joint.

Sabbatical

When leaves start to change color,
so does the vibe of many
Eastern resort communities.

Teachers' autumn retreat approaches.
Forested hills beckon.
Avoid disappointment—

make your reservation early,
don't wait until too late,
or miss blazing leafy adventures

of mathematics like figuring how
many relatives you would have to s
ave to break even.

There is no good reason that your number
is right, but an ounce of algebra
is worth a ton of jive.

About Vachine

Vachine
aka Rolland Vasin

A third-generation American writer, published in the anthologies *WideAwake* and *CoiledSerpent*, among others. Featured at local performance venues, and a reader in open-mics from coast to coast. His poem "read some poems at your link" won third place in the First Angela Consolo Mankiewicz Poetry Prize (2018). He received the Laugh Factory's 1992 "Third Funniest CPA in LA" award. His day job includes auditing children's charities.

The LUMMOX Press was established in 1994 and has published the Little Red Book series and the Lummox Journal. It now publishes chapbooks, a perfect bound book series, a Poetry Anthology & Poetry Contest (annually), and "e-copies" (PDFs) of many of the perfect bound titles.

The goal of the press is to elevate the bar for poetry, while bringing the "word" to an international audience. I am proud to offer this book as part of that effort.

For more information and to see our growing catalog of choices, please go to
www.lummoxpress.com

www.ingramcontent.com/pod-product-compliance
Lightning Source LLC
Chambersburg PA
CBHW031141160426
43193CB00008B/214